Doggin' Orlando

The 31 Best Places
To Hike With Your Dog
In Central Florida

DOUG GELBERT

illustrations by

ANDREW CHESWORTH

CRUDEN BAY BOOKS

There is always a new trail to look forward to...

DOGGIN' ORLANDO: THE 31 BEST PLACES TO HIKE
WITH YOUR DOG IN CENTRAL FLORIDA

Cruden Bay Books
PO Box 467
Montchanin, DE 19710
www.hikewithyourdog.com

International Standard Book Number 978-1-935771-21-0

*"Dogs are our link to paradise...to sit with a dog on a hillside
on a glorious afternoon is to be back in Eden,
where doing nothing was not boring - it was peace."*
- Milan Kundera

Ahead On The Trail

Also...

Introduction

Orlando can be a great place to hike with your dog. Within a short drive your canine adventurer can be climbing ancient dunes that leave him panting, trotting in rolling pinelands, exploring heritage cattle ranches or circling lakes for miles and never lose sight of the water.

I have selected what I consider to be the 30 best places to take your dog for an outing in around Orlando and ranked them according to subjective criteria including the variety of hikes available, dog-friendliness and pleasure of the walks. The rankings include a mix of parks that feature long hikes and parks that contain short walks. Did I miss your favorite? Let us know at *www.hikewithyourdog.com*.

For dog owners it is important to realize that not all parks are open to our best trail companions (see page 15 for a list of parks that do not allow dogs). It is sometimes hard to believe but not everyone loves dogs. We are, in fact, in the minority when compared with our non-dog owning neighbors.

So when visiting a park always keep your dog under control and clean up any messes and we can all expect our great parks to remain open to our dogs. And maybe some others will see the light as well. *Remember, every time you go out with your dog you are an ambassador for all dog owners.*

Grab that leash and hit the trail!
DBG

Hiking With Your Dog

So you want to start hiking with your dog. Hiking with your dog can be a fascinating way to explore Central Florida from a canine perspective. Some things to consider:

🐾 Dog's Health

Hiking can be a wonderful preventative for any number of physical and behavioral disorders. One in every three dogs is overweight and running up trails and leaping through streams is great exercise to help keep pounds off. Hiking can also relieve boredom in a dog's routine and calm dogs prone to destructive habits. And hiking with your dog strengthens the overall owner/dog bond.

🐾 Breed of Dog

All dogs enjoy the new scents and sights of a trail. But some dogs are better suited to hiking than others. If you don't as yet have a hiking companion, select a breed that matches your interests. Do you look forward to an entire afternoon's hiking? You'll need a dog bred to keep up with such a pace, such as a retriever or a spaniel. Is a half-hour enough walking for you? It may not be for an energetic dog like a border collie. If you already have a hiking friend, tailor your plans to his abilities.

🐾 Conditioning

Just like humans, dogs need to be acclimated to the task at hand. An inactive dog cannot be expected to bounce from the easy chair in the den to complete a 3-hour hike. You must also be physically able to restrain your dog if confronted with distractions on the trail (like a scampering squirrel or a pack of joggers). Have your dog checked by a veterinarian before significantly increasing his activity level.

🐾 Weather

Hot humid Florida summers do not do dogs any favors. With no sweat glands and only panting available to disperse body heat, dogs are much more susceptible to heat stroke than we are. Unusually rapid panting and/or a bright red tongue are signs of heat exhaustion in your pet.

Always carry enough water for your hike. Even the prime hiking days of late fall through early spring that don't seem too warm can cause discomfort in dark-coated dogs if the sun is shining brightly. During cold snaps, short-coated breeds may require additional attention.

Trail Hazards

Dogs won't get poison ivy but they can transfer it to you. Some trails are littered with small pieces of broken glass that can slice a dog's paws. Nasty thorns can also blanket trails that we in shoes may never notice. At the beach beware of sand spurs that can often be present in scrubby, sandy areas.

Ticks

You won't be able to spend much time in Florida woods without encountering ticks. All are nasty but the deer tick - no bigger than a pin head - carries with it the spectre of Lyme disease. Lyme disease attacks a dog's joints and makes walking painful. The tick needs to be embedded in the skin to transmit Lyme disease. It takes 4-6 hours for a tick to become embedded and another 24-48 hours to transmit Lyme disease bacteria.

When hiking, walk in the middle of trails away from tall grass and bushes. And when the summer sun fades away don't stop thinking about ticks - they remain active any time the temperature is above 30 degrees. By checking your dog - and yourself - thoroughly after each walk you can help avoid Lyme disease. Ticks tend to congregate on your dog's ears, between the toes and around the neck and head.

Water

Surface water, including fast-flowing streams, is likely to be infested with a microscopic protozoa called *Giardia*, waiting to wreak havoc on a dog's intestinal system. The most common symptom is crippling diarrhea. Algae, pollutants and contaminants can all be in streams, ponds and puddles. If possible, carry fresh water for your dog on the trail - your dog can even learn to drink happily from a squirt bottle.

At the beach, cool sea water will be tempting for your dog but try to limit any drinking as much as possible. Again, have plenty of fresh water available for your dog to drink instead.

🐾 Rattlesnakes and Copperheads, etc.

Rattlesnakes and their close cousins, copperheads, are not particularly aggressive animals but you should treat any venomous snake with respect and keep your distance. A rattler's colors may vary but they are recognized by the namesake rattle on the tail and a diamond-shaped head. Unless cornered or teased by humans or dogs, a rattlesnake will crawl away and avoid striking. Avoid placing your hand in unexamined rocky areas and crevasses and try and keep your dog from doing so as well. Stick to the trail and out of high grass where you can't see well. If you hear a nearby rattle, stop immediately and hold your dog back. Identify where the snake is and slowly back away.

If you or your dog is bitten, do not panic but get to a hospital or veterinarian with as little physical movement as possible. Wrap between the bite and the heart. Rattlesnakes might give "dry bites" where no poison is injected, but you should always check with a doctor after a bite even if you feel fine.

🐾 Black Bears

Are you likely to see a bear while out hiking with your dog? No, it's not likely. It is, however, quite a thrill if you are fortunate enough to spot a black bear on the trail - from a distance.

Black bear attacks are incredibly rare. In the year 2000 a hiker was killed by a black bear in Great Smoky National Park and it was the first deadly bear attack in the 66-year history of America's most popular national park. It was the first EVER in the southeastern United States. In all of North America only 43 black bear mauling deaths have ever been recorded (through 1999).

Most problems with black bears occur near a campground (like the above incident) where bears have learned to forage for unprotected food. On the trail bears will typically see you and leave the area. What should you do if you encounter a black bear? Experts agree on three important things:

1) Never run. A bear will outrun you, outclimb you, outswim you. Don't look like prey.
2) Never get between a female bear and a cub who may be nearby feeding.
3) Leave a bear an escape route.

If the bear is at least 15 feet away and notices you make sure you keep your dog close and calm. If a bear stands on its hind legs or comes closer it may just be trying to get a better view or smell to evaluate the situation. Wave your arms and make noise to scare the bear away. Most bears will quickly leave the area.

If you encounter a black bear at close range, stand upright and make yourself appear as large a foe as possible. Avoid direct eye contact and speak in a calm, assertive and assuring voice as you back up slowly and out of danger.

Alligators

Alligators are found in marshes, swamps, rivers and lakes as well as neighborhood drainage ditches and canals - anywhere you see water is potential gator habitat. Use common sense and do not not allow your dog in waters where alligators may be lurking. Don't walk your dog close to water if you can avoid it.

If you see an alligator on land, just walk your dog away from the area - although they can scurry 30 miles per hour for short distances, alligators do not run down prey on land. They may run on land to escape danger or protect a nest but will not come after you if there is an escape route to the water. Make sure you give him one.

Outfitting Your Dog For A Hike

These are the basics for taking your dog on a hike:

▶ **Collar.**
A properly fitting collar should not be so loose as to come off but you should be able to slide your flat hand under the collar.

▶ **Identification Tags.**
Get one with your veterinarian's phone number as well.

▶ **Bandanna.**
Can help distinguish him from game in hunting season.

▶ **Leash.**
Leather lasts forever but if there's water in your dog's future, consider quick-drying nylon.

▶ **Water.**
Carry 8 ounces for every hour of hiking.

🐾 *I want my dog to help carry water, snacks and other supplies on the trail. Where do I start?*
To select an appropriate dog pack measure your dog's girth around the rib cage. A dog pack should fit securely without hindering the dog's ability to walk normally.

🐾 *Will my dog wear a pack?*
Wearing a dog pack is no more obtrusive than wearing a collar, although some dogs will take to a pack easier than others. Introduce the pack by draping a towel over your dog's back in the house and then having your dog wear an empty pack on short walks. Progressively add some crumpled newspaper and then bits of clothing. Fill the pack with treats and reward your dog from the stash. Soon your dog will associate the dog pack with an outdoor adventure and will eagerly look forward to wearing it.

How much weight can I put into a dog pack?

Many dog packs are sold by weight recommendations. A healthy, well-conditioned dog can comfortably carry 25% to 33% of its body weight. Breeds prone to back problems or hip dysplasia should not wear dog packs. Consult your veterinarian before stuffing the pouches with gear.

How does a dog wear a pack?

The pack, typically with cargo pouches on either side, should ride as close to the shoulders as possible without limiting movement. The straps that hold the dog pack in place should be situated where they will not cause chafing.

What are good things to put in a dog pack?

Low density items such as food and poop bags are good choices. Ice cold bottles of water can cool your dog down on hot days. Don't put anything in a dog pack that can break. Dogs will bang the pack on rocks and trees as they wiggle through tight spots in the trail. Dogs also like to lie down in creeks and other wet spots so seal items in plastic bags. A good use for dog packs when on day hikes around Central Florida is trail maintenance - your dog can pack out trash left by inconsiderate visitors before you.

🐾 *Are dog booties a good idea?*

Although not typically necessary, dog booties can be an asset, especially for the occasional canine hiker whose paw pads have not become toughened. Trails can be rocky and in some places there may be broken glass or roots. Hiking boots for dogs are designed to prevent pads from cracking while trotting across rough surfaces.

🐾 *What should a doggie first aid kit include?*

Even when taking short hikes it is a good idea to have some basics available for emergencies:

- ▶ 4" square gauze pads
- ▶ cling type bandaging tapes
- ▶ topical wound disinfectant cream
- ▶ tweezers
- ▶ insect repellent - no reason to leave your dog unprotected against mosquitoes and biting flies
- ▶ veterinarian's phone number

How To Pet A Dog
Tickling tummies slowly and gently works wonders.
Never use a rubbing motion; this makes dogs bad-tempered.
A gentle tickle with the tips of the fingers is all that is necessary
to induce calm in a dog. I hate strangers who go up to dogs with their
hands held to the dog's nose, usually palm towards themselves.
How does the dog know that the hand doesn't hold something horrid?
The palm should always be shown to the dog and go straight
down to between the dog's front legs and tickle gently with
a soothing voice to accompany the action.
Very often the dog raises its back leg in a scratching movement,
it gets so much pleasure from this.
-Barbara Woodhouse

Low Impact Hiking With Your Dog

Every time you hike with your dog on the trail you are an ambassador for all dog owners. Some people you meet won't believe in your right to take a dog on the trail. Be friendly to all and make the best impression you can by practicing low impact hiking with your dog:

- Pack out everything you pack in.

- Do not leave dog scat on the trail; if you haven't brought plastic bags for poop removal bury it away from the trail and topical water sources.

- Hike only where dogs are allowed.

- Stay on the trail.

- Do not allow your dog to chase wildlife.

- Step off the trail and wait with your dog while horses and other hikers pass.

- Do not allow your dog to bark - people are enjoying the trail for serenity.

- ***Have as much fun on your hike as your dog does.***

The Other End Of The Leash

Leash laws are like speed limits - everyone seems to have a private interpretation of their validity. Some dog owners never go outside with an unleashed dog; others treat the laws as suggestions or disregard them completely. It is not the purpose of this book to tell dog owners where to go to evade the leash laws or reveal the parks where rangers will look the other way at an unleashed dog. Nor is it the business of this book to preach vigilant adherence to the leash laws. Nothing written in a book is going to change people's behavior with regard to leash laws. So this will be the last time leash laws are mentioned, save occasionally when we point out the parks where dogs are welcomed off leash.

Visiting Florida State Parks

State park pet rules: "Pets are permitted in designated day-use areas at ALL Florida State Parks. They must be kept on a hand-held leash that is six-feet or shorter and be well-behaved at all times. Pet owners are required to pick up after their pets and properly dispose of their droppings. Pets are not permitted on beaches or playgrounds, or in bathing areas, cabins, park buildings, or concession facilities."

State forests and wildlife management areas in Florida allow hunting. If you can only hike with your dog in such places during hunting season, outfit yourself and your dog in blaze orange and stick to the trails. Hunting season coincides with prime hiking season after September but often is restricted to specific days of the week so plan your dog's outings accordingly.

The Best of the Best

🐾 **BEST CANINE HIKE TO A VIEW**
Lake Louisa State Park

🐾 **BEST HIKE TO MEET OTHER DOGS**
Shingle Creek Regional Park

🐾 **BEST HIKE TO NOT SEE ANOTHER DOG**
Colt Creek State Park

🐾 **BEST 1-HOUR WORKOUT FOR YOUR DOG**
Catfish Creek State Preserve Park

🐾 **BEST PARK TO FOR YOUR DOG TO SWIM**
Fleet Peeples Park

🐾 **BEST PLACE TO HIKE ALL DAY WITH YOUR DOG**
Hal Scott Regional Preserve and Park

🐾 **PRETTIEST HIKE WITH YOUR DOG**
Hontoon Island State Park

🐾 **BEST HIKE ALONG WATER WITH YOUR DOG**
Little Big Econ State Forest

🐾 **MOST HISTORIC HIKE WITH YOUR DOG**
De Leon Springs State Park

No Dogs

Before we get started on the best places to take your dog, let's get out of the way some of the parks that do not allow dogs at all:

Bernice G. Jackson Park - *Sharpes*

Blanton Park - *Titusville*

Blue Hole Park - *Titusville*

Bourlay Historic Nature Park - *Leesburg*

Central Park - *Winter Haven*

Chain of Lakes - *Titusville*

Circle B Bar Reserve - *Lakeland*

Cuyler Park - *Mims*

Disney Wilderness Preserve - *Kissimmee*

Enchanted Forest Nature Sanctuary - *Titusville*

Fort Christmas Historical Park - *Christmas*

Kelly Park - *Opapka*

Lake Woodruff National Wildlife Refuge -

De Leon Springs

Lyonia Preserve - *Deltona*

Ocala National Forest - all day-use areas

Orlando Wetlands Park - *Christmas*

PEAR Environmental Park trails - *Leesburg*

Pine Island Conservation Area - *Merritt Island*

Split Oak Forest Wildlife and Environmental Area -

St. Cloud

O.K. there were more but that was getting depressing. Let's forget about these and move on to some of the great places where we CAN take our dogs on Orlando area trails...

The 31 Best Places To Hike With Your Dog Around Orlando...

1
Colt Creek
State Park

The Park

Charlie Mac Overstreet began raising beef cattle on this land in the 1930s. More than 1,200 acres of pastureland here grazed a herd of some 1,000 head. After the State bought over 5,000 acres of the Overstreet ranch in 2006 the remaining cattle were driven from the property.

Colt Creek became Florida's 160th state park and one of five management units of the Green Swamp Wilderness Preserve. Second only to the Everglades in wildlife abundance in Florida, the headwaters of the Peace River, Withlacoochee River, Ocklawaha River, and Hillsborough River course through the Green Swamp. Colt Creek is one of the many tributaries that create this hydrological treasure.

The Walks

Colt Creek is the park to head to for big, solitary hikes with your dog. There are over 12 miles of trails here, mostly on wide, grassy road-trails tripping through airy pine flatwoods.

Polk County

Phone Number
- (863) 815-6761

Website
- floridastateparks.org/coltcreek

Admission Fee
- Vehicle entrance fee

Park Hours
- 8:00 a.m. to sunset

Directions
- *Lakeland*; 16 miles north of town. From I-4 take Exit 32 and go north on US 98 for 13 miles to SR 471. Turn right and continue to the park entrance on the right.

A bench is a welcome find for your dog deep in the extensive Colt Creek trail system.

The star walk is the multi-hour excursion on the *Orange Trail* loop that is the only route accessed from the park trailheads. From there you can simply point your dog down the orange blazes or craft a canine hiking day with blue-blazed side trails and cut-offs. Most of your dog's time will be spent with the saw palmetto and longleaf pines but the trails also touch on the expanses of heritage pastureland where your trail dog can channel his inner cattle dog.

Don't overlook the short *Nature Trail* near Mac Lake which wanders through a hardwood hammock with the park's thickest concentration of sabal palms and cypress on a sandy path.

Trail Sense: It's a big park so make sure you bring a trail map that identifies the routes and numbered reference posts.

Dog Friendliness
Dogs are allowed to hike the trails but not in the primitive camps.
Traffic
Horses will share the hiking trails but bikes are permitted only on service roads.
Canine Swimming
No dogs allowed in the lakes.
Trail Time
Don't come to Colt Creek unless you are ready for at least a couple hours of hiking wiht your dog.

2
Little Big Econ
State Forest

The Park

The Little Big Econ State Forest takes its odd name from a mashing of the Little Econlockhatchee River and the larger Econlockhatchee River, a north-flowing, 54-mile-long black-water tributary of the St. Johns River. The State began buying land here for conservation and recreation in 1990 and today the forest sprawls across nearly 10,000 acres in two tracts.

The Walks

The namesake Econlockhatchee River is the star of the canine hiking in the state forest and this is the best streamside hike your dog can take in Central Florida. The most popular way to experience the Econ-

Seminole County

Phone Number
- (352) 732-1225

Website
- floridaforestservice.com/
state_forests/little_big_econ.html

Admission Fee
- Trail fee

Park Hours
- Sunrise to sunset

Directions
- *Oviedo*; 3.3 miles east of town on the right side of CR 426 to reach the Barr Street hiking trailhead. Other trailheads can be accessed by continuing to Old Mims Road and turning right and right again on Snow Hill Road.

lockhatchee is launching from the Barr Street Trailhead using the *Florida National Scenic Trail* to complete the state forest *Kolokee Trail Loop*, a journey of 4.8 miles. The footpath snakes along the heavily vegetated riverbanks on sandy bluffs. A variety of conveyances are available to move your dog across low spots and channel cuts.

The turn-around point is the ram-rod straight *Flagler Trail*, once the railbed of the Okeechobee branch of the Florida East Coast Railway and today a hard-surfaced, multi-use recreational path. As you loop back towards the trailhead you enter the flatwoods and longleaf pine restoration areas. If you opt to extend your dog's hiking day here and try some of the grassy horse trails the wide passages will make it seem as if you are trundling down dog-leg par fours at the local golf club.

Henry Flagler, a failed salt miner, went into the oil refining business with John D. Rockefeller in 1867 and together they built the biggest business empire in the world. On a wedding trip to Florida with his second wife in 1881 the Flaglers visited St. Augustine where they were charmed with the town's Old World Spanish flavor. In short order Flagler gave up day-to-day operations at Standard Oil and set about developing St. Augustine as "the Newport of the South." His vision would soon extend down the Florida peninsula, however, investing $50 million in his railroad and development all the way to Key West by 1912. The Flagler railroad through here was a spur used for lumbering and its trestle (supports still visible) was the first means of crossing the Econlockhatchee River.

Trail Sense: There are alot of trails rambling through Little Big Econ so take a moment to sort them all out. There are maps and blazes and directional signs in the park to help out.

Dog Friendliness
Dogs are allowed to hike in the Little Big Econ State Forest.

Traffic
Mountain bikers have their own trail system here, as do equestrians. *Flagler Trail* can house most anything except motorized vehicles.

Canine Swimming
Several times the trail dips down to sandy beaches on the shores of the Econlockhatchee River for your dog to enjoy.

Trail Time
Two hours to a half-day and more possible.

3
Lake Kissimmee State Park

The Park

This was open range for centuries until the 1940s. During the Civil War cattle raised here were shipped to the Confederate Army. In 1948 William Zipperer bought the land and fenced in a ranch. In 1969 the Zipperer family sold 5,030 acres bounded by Lake Kissimmee to the east, Lake Rosalie to the west and Tiger Lake to the south to the State. The near-virgin land was sculpted into a park with camping and marina facilities and Lakeland architect James Peterson designed board-and-batten park structures to blend into the natural surroundings. All was ready for an August 1977 opening.

Polk County

Phone Number
- (863) 696-1112

Website
- floridastateparks.org/ lakekissimmee

Admission Fee
- Vehicle entrance fee

Park Hours
- 8:00 a.m. to sunset

Directions
- *Lake Wales*; 15 miles east of town. From US 27 South turn left, east, on Chalet Suzanne Road. Continue straight as it becomes Masterpiece Road, which bends to the right. Turn left on Mammoth Grove Road and left on Camp Mack Road to the park entrance on the right.

The Walks

There are more than 13 miles of easy-going hiking trails at Lake Kissimmee, primarily on the white-blazed, 6.7-mile *Buster Island Loop* and the yellow-blazed 6.0-mile *North Loop*. Both visit pine flatwoods and hardwood hammocks where the longleaf pines and oaks are reminders of the days when the area was a busy timber and turpentine center in the late 19th century. Buster Island, named for Billy Buster who was a Seminole Indian run out of the tribe for killing the son of Chief Chippo and exiled here, is the high ground of the park. Don't be put off by the distances - there are several blue-blazed connector trails to fashion less ambitious canine hikes.

Connecting to the *North Loop*, or hiked on its own from the back of the Tiger Cove parking lot, is the 2.8-mile *Gobbler Ridge Scenic Loop*. This high sand ridge leaves the woodlands behind as it snakes out to the grassy shores of Lake Kissimmee. Your dog will trot alternately on sand, dirt and grass roads on this open air exploration where you may well be watched by a bald eagle or osprey.

The Gobbler Ridge Trail will take your dog to the wide-open shores of Lake Kissimmee, the third largest lake in the state of Florida.

Trail Sense: The trails and connectors are well-marked and trail maps are available.

Dog Friendliness
Dogs are welcome on the trails and in the campground.
Traffic
Horses can share some of these trails.
Canine Swimming
Alligators are present in the lakes and Zipperer Canal.
Trail Time
Plan on at least an hour with many more possible.

4
Hickory Bluff Preserve

The Park

American Heritage Rivers were created by an Executive Order from President Bill Clinton in 1997 to provide environmental protection to waterways deemed of economic, historic and cultural distinction. Of the 14 river systems so designated St. Johns River is the only one in the Southeast. In 2003 the Volusia Conservation Lands acquired land on the natural bluff spreading out from the north bank of the St. Johns River to preserve and enhance the rich natural resources found here.

The Walks

This is Central Florida writ on a Terrier scale rather than the Great Dane scale of some of the park's neighbors. Instead of thousands of acres there are only 150 acres here but your dog can still experience oak hammocks, pine flatwoods, cypress domes and floodplain swamps on two scenic trails, each a loop of about one mile. Wave after wave of saw palmetto are punctuated by a catalog collection of Florida pines. Individual sabal palms make dramatic statements in the mid-story as well.

Volusia County

Phone Number
- (386) 740-5261

Website
- volusia.org/growth/hickory.htm

Admission Fee
- None

Park Hours
- Sunrise to sunset

Directions
- *Osteen*; east of town at 598 Guise Road. From CR 415 turn east on New Smyrna Boulevard which quickly becomes Florida Avenue and then Maytown Road. Continue to Guise Road on your right. Turn and continue to the park on the right.

The forest at Hickory Bluff would be impenetrable through the saw palmetto without the well-engineered sand trails.

These are paw-friendly sand-based paths that become increasing pine-straw covered as your dog moves onto the red-blazed loop. The St. Johns River seldom looks as attractive as it does from Hickory Bluff along the blue-blazed *River Trail*.

Trail Sense: There is a mapboard at the trailhead and signposts out in the park although the first crucial junction is unmarked - turn left.

Dog Friendliness
Dogs are welcome on these trails.

Traffic
Horses and bikes are allowed; the former is more likely than the latter which won't be able to handle the soft sand.

Canine Swimming
Alligators are known to frequent the St. Johns River here.

Trail Time
A tail-wagging hour at Hickory Bluff.

5
Hontoon Island State Park

The Park

The Timucuan Indians were the first inhabitants of Hontoon Island that lies between the St. Johns River and the Hontoon Dead River. Later it served as a pioneer homestead, a boat yard, a base for commercial fishing and finally, before the State purchased the 1,650-acre island in 1967, a cattle ranch. Access to this unique oasis is by private boat or park ferry only.

The Walks

Canine hiking on Hontoon Island delivers two distinctly different experiences for your dog. The destination for most adventurers, if one is needed on these inviting island trails, is a series of 2,000-year old mounds of discarded shells about 1.5 miles from the ferry dock. The *Hammock Hiking Natural Trail* is a rolling footpath through pines and broadleaf laurel oaks that earns the Seminole definition for a "hammock" as a shady place. The trail picks its way past fallen arboreal giants and through a lively understory before arriving at the Indian shell mounds by the Hontoon Dead River. The

Volusia County

Phone Number
- (386) 736-5309

Website
- floridastateparks.org/hontoonisland

Admission Fee
- Donations

Park Hours
- 8:00 a.m. to sunset

Directions
- *DeLand*; west of town off SR 44. Following signs, turn onto CR 4110 (Old New York Avenue) and turn left on Hontoon Road (CR 4125). Turn left on River Ridge Road and continue to parking for the ferry dock on the left side.

Access to Hontoon Island is by the tail-friendly park ferry.

return trip can be accomplished on the network of sandy island roads that crisscross the open, pine flatwoods that cover the higher part of Hontoon Island. More Indian artifacts can be explored with your dog in the picnic area where replica totems carved from logs mingle with the sabal palms and oaks.

The Indian shell mounds on Hontoon Island are over 2,000 years old.

Trail Sense: A trail map is available outside the Visitor Center and will be a must-have if you venture onto the five miles of service roads.

Dog Friendliness
Dogs are allowed across the island and on the park ferry.

Traffic
Bikes can use the service roads but don't expect too many trail users.

Canine Swimming
There is easy access to the rivers if you avoid the alligators and fishermen.

Trail Time
At least an hour.

6
Hal Scott Regional Preserve and Park

The Park

Timucuan Indian mounds give evidence of human habitation here going back thousands of years. Early settlers knew this place as Curry Ford where you could cross the Econlockhatchee River when traveling between Central Florida and the Atlantic coast. After the Cheney Highway was constructed in 1924 the traffic disappeared and the cattle moved in to graze on lands that had been timbered and turpentined. Land acquisition for conservation and flood control began here in 1992 and today more than 9,000 acres are owned and managed by the St. Johns River Water Management District and Orange County.

Orange County
Phone Number - (386) 329-4404
Website - sjrwmd.com/recreationguide/halscott
Admission Fee - None
Park Hours - Dawn to dusk
Directions - *Wedgefield*; From SR 520, turn west into the Wedgefield subdivision on Macon Parkway. Turn left on Bancroft Boulevard, right on Meredith Parkway, and left on Dallas Boulevard to the entrance on the right. From Orlando, there is an exit for Dallas Boulevard off the BeeLine Expressway (Route 528) east-bound only.

The Walks

The majority of your dog's hiking day at Hal Scott Preserve will be in sparse pine flatwoods and open prairie where shade is just a rumor so come prepared. The saw palmetto understory is desert-like so views will be long, even for short trail dogs. The vast grasslands are studded with wildflowers poking out as you move along the road-trails of the 4.3-mile *White Loop* where the elevation rarely deviates from between 60-65 feet. Multi-hour explorations will bring you to riparian wetlands and cypress domes along the Econlockhatchee River. The *White Loop* launches a pair of six-mile loops but unless your dog is really loving the wide open spaces you may content yourself with only a short investigation of the floodplain forest along the river by walking a short ways down the *Yellow Loop*.

Even short dogs will enjoy long views from the Hal Scott Preserve trails.

Trail Sense: Your best park map, complete with distances, is downloaded from the website. An information board and maybe trail maps are on-site.

Dog Friendliness
Dogs are allowed on the trails and at the campsites.
Traffic
Horses and bikes also frequent these 19 miles of trails.
Canine Swimming
Your dog can cool down in depression ponds.
Trail Time
At least two hours and a full day of canine hiking available.

7
Lake Louisa
State Park

The Park

The waters of the Green Swamp drain slowly northward through a chain of 13 lakes known as the Palatlakaha, of which Lake Louisa, the southernmost, is the largest. Settlement began in the early 1900s when John and Louise Driggors Hammond established a homestead that included a turpentine still, sawmill, shingle mill and barrel-making operation. A narrow gauge railway hauled logs from the Lake Louisa swamp to the sawmill and steamboats and barges transported goods across Lake Louisa. In 1943 the Bronson family acquired the property and scalped the hillsides for cattle ranching and orange groves, some of which can still be seen above Dixie Lake. The state opened the park, now over 4,000 acres in size, in 1974.

Lake County

Phone Number
- (352) 394-3969

Website
- floridastateparks.org/lakelouisa

Admission Fee
- Vehicle entrance fee

Park Hours
- 8:00 a.m. to sunset

Directions
- *Clermont*; 7 miles south of town. From Route 50 take US 27 south to the park entrance on the right.

The Walks

Lake Louisa boasts a somewhat odd trail system but once you establish a game plan for your dog there is plenty of tail-wagging fun to be had here. Essentially the main hiking route is a 3.5-mile linear trail, blazed in orange, that starts at the ranger station at the highest point on the property and rolls down to the parking lot at the edge of Lake Louisa. This is an ideal park for a two-car shuttle.

Along the way are diversionary loops such as the *Hilltop Loop* where longleaf pines have been re-established and a *Cypress Loop* on the sandy shores of Lake Louisa. Parking is limited to a pair of two-vehicle lots in the middle of the hiking trail system so your dog may define her day here exploring either end of the linear path. Your dog can also test the park hills on 16 miles of horse trails, best accessed at Dixie Lake across Big Creek.

Trail Sense: The trails are meticulously blazed but you will require a trail map to decipher them; the main trail goes by different names as it progresses through the park.

Dog Friendliness
Dogs are welcome on the trails and in the campground.

Traffic
Some of the trails are multi-use.

Canine Swimming
Lake Louisa, approached across glistening white beach sand, is a splendid place for your dog to cool off in the sandy shallows. The tea-colored waters are safe, the lake shallows are stained by the decaying vegetation washed down from the Green Swamp.

Trail Time
Up to a full day possible.

Your dog can look forward to a refreshing cool-down in Lake Louisa after hiking the park trails.

8
Wekiwa Springs State Park

The Park

This area was known as Clay Springs until 1906 when the name was changed to Wekiwa, an interpretation of the Seminole word for "spring of water." Tourists were already making their way to the springs that pour forty-two million gallons of crystal clear water into Wekiwa Springs Run every day to partake in their reputed healing powers.

Early pioneers farmed this land around the springs and it was part of an antebellum cotton plantation before the Civil War. Saw mills, grist mills and turpentine stills all operated here through the years. In the 1930s a group of young hunters began tracking game on the property. Calling themselves the Apopka Sportsmen's Club, membership was by secret ballot and cost $50 for an initiation fee. Annual dues were $15. In 1941 members pooled their money and purchased the land from the Wilson Cypress Company with the mission of practicing conservation and preserving the natural beauty. In 1969 the club's then 50 shareholders voted to sell the land to the state for $2.1 million, accepting a lesser dollar value to keep the property undeveloped.

Orange County

Phone Number
- (352) 360-6675

Website
- floridastateparks.org/ wekiwasprings

Admission Fee
- Vehicle entrance fee

Park Hours
- 8:00 a.m. to sunset

Directions
- *Apopka*; at 1800 Wekiwa Circle. From I-4, take Exit 94 west onto SR 434. After one mile turn right on Wekiwa Springs Road and continue to the park entrance on the right in four miles.

The Walks

For a park that sits across from a gated golf community and gets so crowded it shuts down, you can nonetheless hike with your dog for hours here and never see another trail user. The main hiking trail covers over 13 miles and everything on the canine hiking menu in Central Florida can be found along the way. Your dog will trot through open, sparse pinelands on roomy sand trails, pick her way down jungle-like footpaths thick with sabal palms and navigate through seas of ferns and saw palmetto.

There are options for shortening the canine hike at Wekiwa Springs but any outing with your dog will be a big one. Even if you stay in the campground and never venture into the wilderness you can hike with your

Mill Creek will tempt your dog to come in and cool down after a long Wekiwa Springs hike.

dog on the 1.9-mile spur between Wekiwa Springs and Sand Lake which offers a sampling of the park's wonders from shady paths to longleaf pine-studded scrub.

Trail Sense: A trail map is available at the park and from the website; the trails are reliably blazed and numbered reference posts are at junctions.

Dog Friendliness
Dogs are allowed on the trails but not near the water at Wekiwa Springs or on the *Wet to Dry Nature Trail*.

Traffic
These are multi-use trails but expect hours of solo time with your dog here.

Canine Swimming
The trails touch on lakes and Rock Springs Run where gators lurk; Mill Creek offers a chance for your dog to cool off - and come out muddy.

Trail Time
A full day possible.

9
Catfish Creek
Preserve State Park

The Park

More than 300,000 years ago this was oceanfront property. The sea has long since receded but the prehistoric sand dunes remain to harbor one of Florida's most unique habitats. In 1991 the Allen David Broussard Catfish Creek Preserve State Park was created to protect the rare plants and animals that live among the sandhills and flatwoods of the Lake Wales Ridge. The French-Canadian Broussards were expelled from Nova Scotia in the 1750s and relocated in Louisiana where they raised cattle for ten generations before William J. Broussard bought into a ranch, now the Crescent J Ranch, here in 1969. The park started with a bit more than 1,000 acres and today encompasses more than 8,000 acres between Lake Pierce and Lake Hatchineha.

Polk County

Phone Number
- (863) 696-1112

Website
- floridastateparks.org/catfishcreek

Admission Fee
- None

Park Hours
- 8:00 a.m. to sunset

Directions
- *Haines City*; southeast of town on the east shore of Lake Pierce. Take Route 17 south of town and turn left on Hatchineha Road (Route 542). After eight miles and passing the Poinciana Parkway on your left turn right on Firetower Road to the parking area in three miles on the left.

The Walks

With deep sand trails that call to mind its ancient heritage as oceanside dunes and hilly ascents (views of the surrounding countryside!), only athletic dogs will want to sign on to the canine hiking at Catfish Creek Preserve. For dogs who accept the challenge and make the trek in this visually stunning landscape, however, they will bring back trail tales unlike any other around Orlando.

Right from the parking lot your dog will scramble up a sandy ridge where the desert-like scrub land will spread out before him. There are six miles of hiking trails and another eight miles of horse trails but the soft-sand hiking will make the going seem about 50% longer. Most of your dog's trotting will be on wide road-trails with almost no shade as you wind round shallow ponds and depression marshes and through the scrub and wire grass thickets. The main hiking loop can be sliced by several shortcuts so you can mold this rugged wilderness park to your dog's abilities.

The sand road-trails at Catfish Creek serve your dog long views from some of Florida's highest elevations.

Trail Sense: Trail maps can be had on the website and in a mailbox at the first trail junction (not in the parking lot) - and you will absolutely want one here. Trail junctions are numbered.

Dog Friendliness
Dogs are permitted to hike these challenging trails.
Traffic
No motorized vehicles; horses and
Canine Swimming
The park is peppered with small ponds and depression marshes.
Trail Time
Many hours possible.

Lower Wekiva River Preserve State Park

The Park

The Weikiva River is one of only two rivers in Florida to be designated as a National Wild and Scenic River by the National Park Service. Before state and federal protection arrived, however, the old growth cypress was logged out of the river and floated down to eager sawmills. To preserve six miles of the St. Johns River and the lower four miles of the Wekiva River and Black Water Creek the State of Florida acquired 5,000 acres here in 1976. Today the park covers almost 18,000 acres and is penetrated by 18 miles of multi-use trails.

Seminole County

Phone Number
- (407) 884-2008

Website
- floridastateparks.org/lowerwekivariver

Admission Fee
- None at Route 46 parking lot; $3 user fee at Katie's Landing

Park Hours
- 8:00 a.m. to sundown

Directions
- *Sanford*; nine miles west on the north side of Route 46. For Katie's Landing continue a short way on Route 46 to Wekiva Park Drive and turn right to the parking lot.

The Walks

The primo walk at Lower Wekiva River-Southeast Unit is the *Katie's/LW Loop* that is blazed in red and covers 4.5 miles through a thickly wooded dry hammock and pine flatlands. The route, that takes advantage of wide, sand roads, can be accessed from either Katie's Landing on the Wekiva River or via a half-mile connector from Route 46. If your dog prefers the shield of the leafy canopy to the open pine scrub you can confine your canine hiking to the two-mile, figure-eight *Sandhill Nature Trail* that is blazed in white and shares the passage with the orange-blazed *Florida Trail*. Seldom crowded, this sandy path littered in pine straw will prove a delight for any level of canine hiker. Backpackers and dogs looking for an all-day hike can visit the park's Northwest Unit (east of Route 44 via Swift Road) where over ten miles of trails await in a series of long loops.

Trail Sense: The best trail map for distances in Central Florida is available on site - you can select exactly how far you want to hike with your dog at Lower Wekiva River Preserve down to the tenth-of-a-mile.

The trotting on the Sandhill Nature Trail is so agreeable your dog may want to go around twice.

Dog Friendliness

Dogs are welcome to hike these trails.

Traffic

These are multi-use trails so you can chance to see a horse, a bike or even a park vehicle.

Canine Swimming

Alligators are present but your dog can slip in and cool off at Katie's Landing, which is an excellent launch site for a canoe trip on the Wekiva River with your dog.

Trail Time

Anywhere from an hour on up.

11
Palm Bluff
Conservation Area

The Park

Historically, the standard Central Florida activities of timbering and cattle ranching went on here but these woods also supported the Russell Alligator Farm, one of 57 farms licensed by the State back in the 1990s to raise the reptiles for their hides and meat. Apparently operators wanted more eggs than their herd of 4,500 gators were producing. Using aircraft launched from two airstrips on the property alligator nests along the St. Johns River were spotted and then raided by airboat. The illegal poaching ring collected hundreds of eggs a week until the operation was uncovered by wildlife officials in 1992. Some $20 million in Florida Forever funds were used in 2009 to acquire 3,321 acres around the Deep Creek basin, a tributary of the Middle St. Johns River.

Volusia County
Phone Number - (386) 329-4404
Website - None
Admission Fee - None
Park Hours - Sunrise to sunset
Directions - *Osteen*; north of town on the east side of CR 415.

The Walks

You say you want to go for a long walk with your dog in the woods? You have come to the right place. The marquee canine hike at Palm Bluff is the *Red Loop Trail* that, with a half-mile connector from the trailhead, covers seven miles of mostly shady flatwoods. The namesake palms are congregated near Deep Creek near the back of the loop and much of your early going will be in pine plantations. The southern leg of the loop passes through the remnants of the alligator farm with the overgrown airstrips and four artificial holding ponds. Other relics on the property include a cabbage palm cabin that was constructed in the 1980s as a hunt cabin. If your dog is just hitting his stride on these wide jeep trails after an hour and the Deep Creek isn't living up to its name, you can add the 2.1-mile *Yellow Loop* to your journey. For canine hikers who aren't seeking such a full day there is a *White Loop* at the *Red Loop* trailhead that runs through mostly wetlands and will limit your dog's fun at Palm Bluff to two miles.

**Past pine plantations help shape
the Pine Bluff forestscape for your
dog's trail day here.**

Trail Sense: The trails are reliably blazed but there are more pathways out there than are shown on the map (available on site) so stay alert.

Dog Friendliness
Dogs are allowed on the trails.
Traffic
The length of the trails are better suited to equestrians so don't be surprised if your dog is sharing the trail with horses.
Canine Swimming
Deep Creek, ditches and depression ponds stand ready to cool down your dog on a hot day.
Trail Time
Many hours possible.

12
Ocala National Forest

The Park

On November 24, 1908, President Theodore Roosevelt designated 202,000 acres of scrub as national forest lands, today known as the Ocala National Forest, a derivative of the Timucuan Indian term meaning "fair land" or "big hammock." It was the first national forest east of the Mississippi River and the second within the Continental United States. Dense sand pine, xeric oak scrub and infertile, dry sandy soil made the Ocala Forest a poor choice for settlement and agriculture. The sand pine here is the largest concentration in the world. Today the Ocala Forest covers approximately 607 square miles - exactly half the size of the state of Rhode Island.

Seminole County+

Phone Number
- (352) 236-0288

Website
- fs.usda.gov/main/ocala

Admission Fee
- Vehicle fee in day-use areas

Park Hours
- Sunrise to sunset

Directions
- *Altoona*; east of town on CR 42 for the Clearwater Recreation Area. For Alexander Springs Recreation Area take US 19 north of Altoona to CR 445 and turn right (paved all the way). For Juniper Springs take US 19 north to Route 40 and go west to the entrance on the right.

The Walks

Dogs are not allowed in the day-use areas of the Ocala National Forest which puts a serious crimp in day hiking opportunities for your best trail companion. The nearest hiking at Ocala to Orlando is at the Clearwater Lake Recreation Area where you can jump onto the *Florida National Scenic Trail* and hike as long as your dog's tail keeps wagging before turning around. Also available here is the *Paisley Woods Bicycle Trail* that rolls ten miles on piney sandhills to the Alexander Springs Recreation Area and loops back. There is a short connector that divides the 22-mile trip into a pair of 11-mile loops, digestible on a single canine hike. Unlike many of the bike trails in Central Florida this one uses single-track passages through the longleaf

pines so stay alert to step your dog aside - it is a bike trail first. Of course, as with any national forest, your dog can make his own fun here with a nose to exploring the jeep roads that riddle the vast woodland.

Trail Sense: The trails are blazed which will serve you until you decide to wander onto forest roads.

Dog Friendliness
Dogs are not allowed in the day-use areas of Ocala National Forest.

Traffic
If you find the desingated trails too crowded you can disappear down a forest road.

Canine Swimming
No swimming in the day-use area springs but there are more than 600 natural ponds and lakes in the Ocala National Forest.

Trail Time
Days and days and days.

13
Seminole
State Forest

The Park

The Seminole State Forest is a 27,000-acre link in the Wekiva River Basin that is the largest contiguous undeveloped landmass in Central Florida. Since 1990 this chunk of protected land has been under the stewardship of the Florida Forest Service which promotes resource management and recreation, including hunting. Hiking is allowed in the forest during the pursuit of small game and turkey which only fills less than five weeks during the year. Hunting dates are prominently displayed on the website to plan accordingly.

Lake County

Phone Number
- (352) 360-6675

Website
- floridaforestservice.com/
state_forests/seminole.html

Admission Fee
- Vehicle parking fee

Park Hours
- 8:00 a.m. to sunset

Directions
- *Sorrento*; two entrances east of town. The north entrance (Cassia Trailhead) is off SR 44 at Brantley Branch Road and the south entrance (Bear Pond Trailhead) is off SR 46 at Wekiva River Road.

The Walks

The *Florida National Scenic Trail* that meanders from Pensacola to Miami runs 7.5 miles down the spine of the Seminole Forest and forms the backbone of your dog's hiking day here. To sample the trail you can simply point your trail dog to the orange blazes and go as far as he wants before retracing your steps to the trailhead or use the *Florida Trail* as a jumping off point for the two main hiking loops in the forest.

From the Bear Pond Trailhead leave the *Florida Trail* for a six-mile spin on the white-blazed *Lower Wekiva Loop* that is wedged between the Blackwater Creek and Wekiva River. The entire canine hike will cover over 10 miles with minimal opportunities for aborting your dog's trip so set off mentally prepared for the challenge. From the Cassia Trailhead your destination is the *North Sulphur Island Loop* that will cover over eight miles but with more opportunity to lessen the journey on service roads and equestrian trails. Either way, your dog's long walk through these woods will shift seamlessly from bottom-land forests to sand pine scrub. A State Forest Use Permit will let you drive to North Sulphur Island but why take away half of your trail dog's good times in Seminole State Forest?

Trail Sense: A trail map is available at the trailhead and if you plan any hiking away from the *Florida Trail*, don't lose it.

Your dog can cool off in Bear Pond after a long hike in the Seminole State Forest.

Dog Friendliness
Dogs are welcome throughout the Seminole State Forest.
Traffic
These are multi-use trails but expect hours of solo time with your dog here.
Canine Swimming
The park is lubricated by several streams although they won't play a big part in your dog's hiking day here.
Trail Time
Many, many hours.

Gator Creek Reserve

The Park

The Green Swamp - more than a half-million acres strong - rises up to 132 feet above sea level and the plateau acts like a sponge, retaining rainwater which drains across the surface to create the headwaters of four major rivers: the Withlacoochee, the Ocklawaha, the Hillsborough and the Peace. In the 1970s the network of wetlands, flatlands and low ridges became a priority for protection to preserve the quality and quantity of Florida's freshwater supply. Gator Creek, which was drained and diverted by the Gator Creek Canal beginning in the 1940s, saves over 2,700 acres as part of the Polk County Environmental Lands Program.

The Walks

Any type of canine hiking day is in the offing on the series of stacked loops that comprise the Gator Creek Reserve trail system. The primo attraction is the park's cypress dome which is explored on a half-mile paved path

Polk County

Phone Number
- (863) 534-7377

Website
- governmentrecoverygrants.org/explore/gator-creek-reserve/

Admission Fee
- None

Park Hours
- 6:00 a.m. to 6:30 p.m. (EST)
  5:30 a.m. to 8:00 p.m. (DST)

Directions
- *Lakeland*; north of town. From I-4 take Exit 32 and go north on US 98 to the entrance on the right about one mile after the road narrows from four lanes to two.

The soft, pine straw-strewn trails in Gator Creek Reserve are a delight for any dog to trot on.

that loops around the freshwater swamp. No one really knows the purpose of the knobby "knees" that radiate from cypress trees but the best guess is they enable often submerged cypress root systems to breathe. These cypress ponds are found only in central Florida.

The hiking trails are accessed down a lumber-lined, stony path that soon gives way to paw-friendly natural trails through the pine flatwoods. The woodlands are often lush enough to shade your dog as he rambles along. The full *Piney Wood Trail* covers two miles but can be sliced to a mile for novice trail dogs. Ambitious canine hikers can cross the remnant of Gator Creek that was long ago drained to allow cattle to graze and pick up more cypress swamps and oak-speckled upland forests on the three-mile *Deer Run Trail*.

Trail Sense: There are trail maps available at the parking lot kiosk and the maps are stapled to posts at trail junctions in the park.

Dog Friendliness
Dogs are allowed to hike these trails.

Traffic
Bikes are also permitted to use Gator Creek Preserve.

Canine Swimming
This is a park for canine hikers, not canine swimmers.

Trail Time
Anything from a leg-stretcher to several hours available for your dog.

15

Rock Springs Run State Reserve

The Park

In 1893, A. E. and H. S. Wilson of Saginaw, Michigan bought the Noah J. Tilghman & Son sawmill in Palatka, up in Putnam County. The mill primarily processed cypress lumber. Renamed the Wilson Cypress Company, operations expanded and at its peak, it was the second largest cypress mill in the world. To feed the beast, massive old-growth cypress was harvested along the Wekiva River and the Rock Springs Run and shipped to the St. Johns River on elevated tram roads. By the early 1940s the river basin was logged out and the sawmill closed in 1944. With an eye to protecting the watershed and preserving a wildlife-rich habitat, land was first acquired here by the State of Florida in 1983.

Orange/Lake Counties

Phone Number
- (407) 884-2008

Website
- floridastateparks.org/rockspringsrun

Admission Fee
- Vehicle parking fee

Park Hours
- 8:00 a.m. to 6:00 p.m.

Directions
- *Sorrento*; from I-4, take Exit 101C onto SR 46 west and go ten miles to the entrance road on the left.

The Walks

This is the Godzilla of Orlando-area trail systems. Here are some numbers: 13,700 acres of land, 14 miles of hiking trails, 17 miles of equestrian trails, 27 miles of canoe trails. All of it is completely undeveloped and when you bring your dog take heed of the park admonition to "Take plenty of water, a compass and a map." There are three parking sites from which to launch your dog's Rock Springs Run adventure from the lone park road: the hiking trails from Site 1; the bike trails from Site 2 and the horse trails from Site 3. The main hiking loop here is called the *Lake Loop*, and although your dog can smell the water he will never see it. It is an honest three-mile trek with many, many more miles possible. After about a half-mile of single-

-track footpaths through thick saw palmetto and a mixed forest you will join the horse and bike trails in the wide open pine scrub where the view of the scattered longleaf pines won't change for hours. This is easy trotting for your dog, however, often on the 12-foot wide, packed sand former logging roads.

This is the view your dog can enjoy for hours on the old logging roads in Rock Springs Run Reserve.

Trail Sense: There is a trail map brochure available at the trailhead but it is a mash-up of colored squares and circles that provide no sense of proportion to the vastness of the property. Your better bet is to study the hand-drawn map on the information board and, better yet, snap a picture of it with your smartphone to take with you. Once the paw meets the ground there are mile markers and directional blazes to heed.

Dog Friendliness
Dogs are allowed on the trails but not in the primitive camping area.
Traffic
Mostly multi-use trails, save for the introductory hiking trails into the system.
Canine Swimming
Only the most athletic dogs will make their way to the oak-shaded crystal waters of Rock Springs Run.
Trail Time
At least an hour and many more.

16

Canaveral Marshes Conservation Area

The Park

The St. Johns River is the longest in Florida - 310 miles. And it is in no hurry to travel from its headwaters in the marshes of Indian River to its mouth in the Atlantic Ocean at Jacksonville. The total drop in elevation is less than 30 feet or less than an inch a mile, making it one of the "laziest" rivers in the world. As it flows through here it is practically whitewater - 2.5 inches of drop per mile. Back around 1912 Edgar W. Ellis formed a consortium known as the Titusville Fruit and Farm Lands Company hoping to drain the marshland in the St. Johns River valley and sell it as cropland. Ellis and his mates bought up 22,500 acres of land and set about digging a drainage canal. All went well in the sand ridges in these marshes but when they reached the coquina rock ridge to the east near Indian River the equipment broke down and the money ran out. The canal never reached a usable depth and was abandoned. When the St. Johns River Water Management District purchased the Canaveral Marshes it was to protect the floodplain, not drain it.

Brevard County

Phone Number
- (386) 329-4404

Website
- floridaswater.com/recreation-guide/canaveralmarshes

Admission Fee
- None

Park Hours
- Dawn to dusk

Directions
- *Titusville*; west of town. Three miles west of I-95, Exit 215 on the Cheyney Highway, Route 50. There is minimal parking at the Conservation lot. There is also access through the Great Outdoors R.V. Resort, two miles to the east. Let them know at the gate you want to use the trails and you will get a parking pass.

The Walks

The Carneval Marshes serve up a potpourri of canine hiking opportunities along dikes and mucky trails and sandy footpaths. One popular destination is the Paw Paw Mound (head down the road from the Route 50

48

parking lot) at the St. Johns River. The artifact-laden Indian relic soars 10-12 feet above its surroundings - high enough in Brevard county to achieve recognition as "a summit" and warrant a United States Geologic Survey marker. Paw Paw Mound is about a mile from the trailhead, across the old Ellis Canal (via a bridge skittish dogs may not embrace).

Your dog will share the Carneval Marshes trails with grazing cattle.

Other explorations in the Carneval Marshes come via the Florida Trail Association's miles of trails. Much of the 6,741 acres here are active cattle pastures and you can expect to see cows - alive and not so alive - roaming the grasslands during your dog's hiking day here.

Trail Sense: The park may not be reliably blazed - best to come with an explorer's heart.

Dog Friendliness
Dogs are allowed to trot these trails.
Traffic
Mostly foot traffic but bikes and horses can also use the roads and trails.
Canine Swimming
Alligators frequent the Ellis Canal and the St. Johns River.
Trail Time
Up to a half-day of exploration in the Carneval Marshes.

17
Saddle Creek Park

The Park

In 1881 Captain Francis LeBaron was surveying the lower Peace River for a United States Army Corps of Engineers canal when he began to find prehistoric fossils in the sand bars. Noticing a phosphatase quality to the fossils LeBaron packed up nine barrels and shipped them to the Smithsonian Institution for analysis. Turns out he had stumbled onto the world's largest deposit of phosphate rock which came to be known as the Bone Valley Deposit. Here at Saddle Creek, the upper-most tributary of the Peace River, high grade phosphate - a key ingredient in agriculture fertilizers - was found close to the surface. The Coronet Fertilizer Company aggressively extracted the ore between 1960 and 1978 before donating 6,058 played-out acres to the State in 1982. Using funds for reclamation, the clay pits were filled to create lakes which were stuffed with largemouth bass, panfish, and black crappie. The rims of the mining pits were formulated into hiking trails and Saddle Creek Park and Tenoroc ("Coronet" spelled backwards) Fish Management Area created.

Polk County

Phone Number
- (407) 742-7800

Website
- saddlecreekpark.com

Admission Fee
- None for Saddle Creek Park; $3 for Tenoroc FMA

Park Hours
- 5:00 a.m. to 10:00 p.m. for Saddle Creek Park; sunrise to sunset for Tenoroc FMA, Friday-Monday only

Directions
- *Lakeland*; From I-4 take Exit 38 south on Route 33. Bear left on Route 659 (North Combee Road). Turn left on Morgan Combee Road into the park and turn left to trailhead parking.

The Walks

After bounding from the car in Saddle Creek Park your dog will be confronted with a choice of trailheads. To the right is the free *Nature Trail*, a linear 1.2-mile ramble that hooks around a series of lakes on a commodiously wide path. Your dog will enjoy a bit of elevation change here before the trail dead-ends. Ignore the narrow side paths that are souvenirs of scout work and likely overgrown.

More meat-and-potatoes hiking awaits your dog on the pay-to-play Tenoroc trails. Here narrow footpaths lead up and down the spoil mounds and along reclaimed lakes to an observation tower with scenic views. Further exploration comes for an extra mile on the *Flatwoods Trail* where,

Your dog will find some of Central Florida's shadiest hiking at Saddle Creek - even hiking through tunnels of vegetation.

unlike the *Nature Trail* and *Lake Loop* that are among central Florida's shadiest walks, the hiking is much more exposed.

Trail Sense: The Tenoroc trails are blazed and there are just enough markings on the *Nature Trail* to get you started. No take-along maps here.

Dog Friendliness
Dogs are allowed to hike in both parks and stay in the campground.
Traffic
Hiking only; no bikes and no vehicles and no horses.
Canine Swimming
Alligators are present in the many lakes.
Trail Time
Allow two to three hours to complete all three trails.

18
De Leon Springs State Park

The Park

If Spanish explorer Juan Ponce de Leon actually did discover the mythical Fountain of Youth, this may have been the place. But settlers in the early 1800s had no time for such legends - they were busy planting sugar cane and cotton. Twice the mills were sacked, once during the Second Seminole Indian War and again during the Civil War by Union troops in 1864 in Birney's Raid. By the 1880s the railroad had reached town and the springs evolved into a winter resort. In 1982 the State acquired the property, transforming De Leon Springs from a tourist attraction to a public park.

Volusia County

Phone Number
- (386) 985-4212

Website
- floridastateparks.org/ deleonsprings

Admission Fee
- Vehicle admission fee

Park Hours
- 8:00 a.m. to sunset

Directions
- *DeLand*; north of town. From I-4 take Exit 114 and follow US 17 north into town. Turn left on Ponce De Leon Boulevard and continue to the park across the railroad tracks.

The Walks

Most visitors to De Leon Springs never walk beyond the half-mile paved *Nature Trail* that loops peaceably down into a flood plain hammock with enchanting hardwoods, pines and cypress trees on display. Maybe they will wander onto the quarter-mile, natural surface trail that leads to Monkey Island where monkeys lived during the park's days as a tourist attraction. But few will step off the macadam onto the *Wild Persimmon Hiking Trail*, where the persimmons are not the only thing that is wild.

Your canine adventurer will find one of her most challenging hikes here on the 4.2-mile balloon-style trail with a long entrance string to the loop. Frequently wet, planks and low bridges help with the crossing of the flood plain. This is among the rootiest paths your dog will negotiate in Central Florida, courtesy of a forest thick with mature and emerging sable palms. The jungle-like ambiance gives way only briefly to abandoned groves and agricultural fields. When your dog re-emerges back onto the paved path she can report on a De Leon Springs experience unfamiliar to nearly all other park guests.

"Old Methuselah" is a cypress tree over 500 years old, somehow dodging the woodsman's axe.

Trail Sense: It is not obvious by park signage but the trailhead for the *Wild Persimmon Trail* is in the middle of the *Nature Trail.*

Dog Friendliness
Dogs are not allowed down by the springs but can hike the trails.
Traffic
Foot traffic only on the trails.
Canine Swimming
None.
Trail Time
Allow two hours to complete the *Wild Persimmon Trail.*

19

Seminole Ranch
Conservation Area

The Park

In 1981, the Florida Legislature created the Water Management Lands Trust Fund, funded from documentary stamp tax revenues from real estate transactions, for the acquisition and restoration of water resources. To date, the Save Our Rivers Program has purchased 1.7 million acres of land and 12 miles of the St. Johns River here was the first acquisition of the program. Today 29,145 acres are protected on both sides of the river. The 6,000 acres to the west of the St. Johns River are part of the Wildlife Management Area where hunting is allowed; no hunting is permitted on the east side.

several counties

Phone Number
- (386) 329-4404

Website
- sjrwmd.com/recreationguide/seminoleranch

Admission Fee
- None

Park Hours
- Dawn to dusk

Directions
- *Christmas*; northeast of town. For the Conservation Area take Hatbill Road south of SR 46 (marked for Hatbill Park). For the Wildlife Management Area take SR 50 to CR 420 north and turn right on Wheeler Road.

The Walks

Canine exploring may be more apropos than canine hiking at Seminole Ranch, especially in the wet season. The best organized hiking is along the 4+ miles of the orange-blazed *Florida Trail* through the Wildlife Management Area that hopscotches among wide open pastureland, marshy riverland (planks and bridges help with the squishy places) and wooded hammocks.

Your dog will alternate between open pastureland and dense woodland on a romp through Seminole Ranch.

Bonus

In Central Florida it is seldom a problem getting your dog into a campground but it is not always simple to get your dog to a campground, especially a primitive site. At Seminole Ranch, along Hatbill Road is a primitive site within a few hundred yards of the parking area.

The park's white-blazed trails can be used to shorten or extend your dog's hiking day on the hunting grounds.

In the Conservation Area south of SR 46 you will find trailheads, although not necessarily parking, at 1.1 and 2.3 miles down the sand ribbon that is Hatbill Road. A dedicated parking area doesn't arrive for four miles. Once on the ground there is a quiltwork of roads and sandy single-track to take your dog through everything Central Florida has to offer in the way of pines, palmettos, oaks and wetlands along with a special sprinkling of salt water springs that support species not found anywhere else in the St. Johns River basin.

After a day of exploring your dog will welcome a convenient campsite like the one at Seminole Ranch Conservation.

Trail Sense: If you are more comfortable with blazed trails, head for the Wildlife Management Area at Seminole Ranch.

Dog Friendliness
Dogs are allowed to use these trails in and out of hunting season.

Traffic
Mostly foot traffic; motorized vehicles are not allowed.

Canine Swimming
Your dog will find lakes and streams - and sometime trails - for splashing in Seminole Ranch.

Trail Time
A few hours to a full weekend.

20

Shingle Creek Regional Park

The Park

Shingle Creek is a small waterway that is considered to be the northern-most headwaters of the Everglades watershed. It got its name from the cypress trees that lined the bank in the late 1800s that were used to make wood shingles.

Tenneseee-born Millard Grady Babb migrated to Central Florida in his late teens in 1917. Babb became a citrus grower and cattle rancher here for the better part of 80 years. After he died in 1996 at the age of 95 his son was diagnosed with skin cancer and could no longer work the groves. The property was sold to the Trust of Public Land with most of the $5 million price tag being picked up with four grants from the Florida Communities Trust. The park along the Shingle Creek corridor then opened in 2009.

Osceola County

Phone Number
- (407) 742-7800

Website
- osceola.org/parks/160-3273-0/shingle_creek_regional_park.cfm

Admission Fee
- None

Park Hours
- 8:00 a.m. to 5:00 p.m. (EST)
  8:00 a.m. to 7:00 p.m. (DST)

Directions
- *Kissimmee*; at 4266 West Vine Stree (US 192) for Steffee Landing. For Babb Landing go to Old Vineland Road just to the west and turn right on Babb Road to the park entrance on the right.

The Walks

Severed by one of the world's busiest tourist highways, seven miles from Disney World, and under the flight path of Kissimmee Municipal Airport, Shingle Creek Regional Park manages to serve your dog a slice of pre-Disney Florida. There is access to the park on the north and south side of US 192, each with a linear trail along the Shingle Creek. Unless you are canoeing with your dog on the shallow waters of the creek the two park segments are unconnected.

**The park features the remnants
of an historic citrus operation.**

**Your dog will find as much fun
off trail as on at Shingle Creek.**

The park trails are serpentine ribbons of crushed gray clay but your dog is likely to have just as good a time trotting on the wide grassy shoulders and romping through the orange grove. Canine hiking at Babb Landing is completely wide open; trees are introduced into your dog's adventure at Steffee Landing south of US 192.

Trail Sense: There is a mapboard at the parking lot which will get you properly oriented to this park.

Dog Friendliness
Dogs are allowed to hike in Shingle Creek Park.
Traffic
This is a splendid place to hike and meet other dogs.
Canine Swimming
There is easy access to Shingle Creek at the canoe launch.
Trail Time
A leisurely hour can be found with your dog in each segment of the park.

21
Lake Monroe Conservation Area

The Park

In the late 1800s Hezekiah and Susan Osteen came here to run cattle in the floodplains of a "flow-through" wide spot of the St. Johns River that came to be known as Lake Monroe. The area was known as Saulsville at the time for one-time Confederate agent George Sauls who homesteaded here. The Osteens would have ten children just like their good friends the Saulses. But nine of the Sauls' children were daughters so by 1882 the town was known as Osteen where Hekekiah served as sheriff, tax collector and a general store proprietor.

In 1987, after more than 100 years in the family, Minnie Beck Kratzert was ready to sell the ranch. Volusia County wanted the 3,248-acre property but couldn't come up with the entire $1.5 million asking price. When an Orlando developer entered the bidding with a $2 million offer the county partnered with the St. Johns River Water Management District to seal the deal. It was the beginning of a rocky relationship.

The county wanted just 200 acres of the parcel to build some ballfields and a playground and some picnic pavilions. But even that small slice of the old Osteen cattle ranch was seen as too much development by the water district conservationists. For nine years nothing happened here until the county accepted another parcel from the adjoining 4,411-acre Beck Ranch, now known as the Brickyard Slough Tract, that was acquired for $3 million in 1995.

Volusia County

Phone Number
- (386) 329-4404

Website
- sjrwmd.com/recreationguide/lakemonroe

Admission Fee
- None

Park Hours
- Sunrise to sunset

Directions
- *Sanford*; northeast of town. Take CR 415 north of SR 46 across the St. Johns River to the Brickyard Slough Tract parking area on the right. Across CR 415, take Reed Ellis Road for the Kratzert Tract trails on the left. Another half-mile up CR 415 turn right on Lemon Bluff Road for that trailhead.

The Walks

There are nine miles of canine hiking on tap at Lake Monroe from a variety of launch points, mostly on open land cleared and planted for cattle grazing. These are big walks on sandy-grassy roads normally traversed by horse or bike but your dog can happily join in. The main loop covers over three miles, best reached by a 15-minute hike in from Lemon Bluff Road. It can also be joined

If it looks like a cow would be at home here it is because they have been for well over 100 years.

by a longer route off CR 415 that penetrates the Brickyard Slough down to grand oaks on the shore of the St. Johns River. In recent years the Kratzert Tract on the west side of CR 415 has been opened to hunting your dog can find a woodsy loop here for 1.4 miles on the *White Trail* and deeper explorations probe this area of mostly wetlands.

Trail Sense: Trail maps are available online and on site to help you decipher the various trailheads and their destinations. Diamond shields lead the way out on the trail.

Dog Friendliness

Dogs are allowed on the trails.

Traffic

Horse and bikes are allowed on these multi-use trails but no motorized vehicles.

Canine Swimming

The trails wind by depression ponds, although they are sometimes fenced off, and down to the St. Johns River. Property descriptions never fail to mention the "large number of alligators."

Trail Time

You can do a canine hike at Lake Monroe that lasts less than one hour or spend most of the day on the trails.

22
Tiger Bay
State Forest

The Park

Park literature tells us that Tiger Bay State Forest is named for its largest physiographic feature, Tiger Bay. No word on how Tiger Bay, a yawning swamp nestled between two historic dunes, got its fearsome name. The most prominent land owner here was Consolidated Tomoka Land Company who began buying up land here in 1912. Historic uses of the tract include cattle grazing, turpentine production, timber management, hunting and apiary use. During that time most of the land was clearcut except for spots in the loblolly bay swamps. Sun Oil Company had an oil and gas lease on a portion of the property from 1941 to 1950 but nothing came of that. The first chunks of Tiger Bay State Forest were acquired in 1979 using Environmentally Endangered Lands Program funds and today it covers 27,330 acres. In 2002 almost 5,000 more acres was purchased next door from Plum Creek Timberlands for the Clark Bay Conservation Area.

Volusia County

Phone Number
- (386) 226-0250

Website
- floridaforestservice.com/state_forests/tiger_bay

Admission Fee
- Parking fee for recreation area

Park Hours
- Sunrise to sunset

Directions
- *Daytona Beach*; seven miles west on the north side of US 92. The entrance for Clark Bay Conservation Area is off Old Daytona Road to the west.

The Walks

Miles of trails and dirt roads are available for canine hiking in Tiger Bay and Clark Bay. More than half of the forest burned during wind-blown wildfires in 1998 so you will be experiencing various states of regeneration among the dominant slash and longleaf pines as you wander with your dog. The only formal canine hiking here is along the two-mile *Buncombe Hill Hiking Trail* that leaves from an old boy scout camp at Indian

Lake, a 66-acre sinkhole, and meanders through a lightly forested sand ridge that was once the home of a turpentine camp. Chips of clay turpentine pots called "Herty cups" can still be seen on the ground. At Clark Bay there is a five-mile balloon trail on an easy-going mix of open scrubland and wetlands.

Trail Sense: There are park maps that will guide you around the property.

Dog Friendliness
Dogs are allowed to hike through the forest.

Traffic
Motorized vehicles are not allowed off the park roads; foot traffic only on the *Buncombe Hill Hiking Trail*.

Canine Swimming
The forest ponds and lakes are home to alligators.

Trail Time
Many hours possible.

23

Buck Lake Conservation Area

The Park

The tale of land use around Buck Lake is a familiar Florida tale: timber and turpentine production and cattle ranching. Almost 10,000 acres of woodlands and wetlands have now been rescued by the St. Johns River Water Management District, which is actively managing for habitat preservation and recreational activities consistent with conservation.

The Walks

There are several ways to order from the canine hiking menu at Buck Lake. If your dog is only hungry for appetizers you can sample the park's delights with a short ramble at both the East and West trailheads. The *Yellow Loop* at the eastern end of the park travels through a piney sand ridge for 1.2 miles and you then move over to the western end where Buck Lake awaits. Here your canine hike begins with a mundane trot down a service road under utility lines. But when you turn for the marsh lake the trail morphs into one of the prettiest strolls for your dog in Central Florida - a wide,

Volusia/Brevard counties

Phone Number
- (386) 329-4404

Website
- sjrwmd.com/recreationguide/bucklake

Admission Fee
- None

Park Hours
- Dawn to dusk

Directions
- *Mims*; west of town. From I-95 take Exit 223 west on SR 46. The East Trailhead is one mile on the right; the West Trailhead is 6.5 miles further along on the right.

The trail to the Buck Lake observation tower is like a garden stroll for your dog.

grassy path rimmed with young pines and sabal palms. Your destination is a wooden observation tower which your dog can climb for extended views across Buck Lake. The journey from parking lot to tower is about one mile.

The trail entrees are meaty hiking loops in the center of the Conservation Area, accessed from either end. If you have a car shuttle it will be a hike with your dog of 7.6 miles. If you walk a loop from either end you sign on for a trip of at least 8.5 miles. All your dog's hiking here is easy going on flat jeep roads surfaced in clay and shell.

Cooling off in Buck Lake after a hot day on the trails.

Trail Sense: An excellent trail map will lay the park out for you.

Dog Friendliness
Dogs are welcome to explore these trails.
Traffic
No motorized vehicles and little competition for these trails deep into the loops.
Canine Swimming
The edges of Buck Lake are easy for your dog to walk into.
Trail Time
A few hours to a full day's canine hiking.

24

Geneva Wilderness Area

The Park

This property was originally owned by the Boy Scouts of America who used it for a campground and environmental education. The 180-acre site was purchased through the Seminole County Natural Lands Program that was established in 1990. A nature center, named for long-time Seminole County cattle rancher and member of the Florida Agricultural Hall of Fame, Ed Yarborough, was opened for folks to learn about nature by experiencing it.

The Walks

The park boasts several miles of canine hiking opportunity, primarily on the series of loops that encircle a flatwoods pond. The red-blazed path traverses a transitional area between open scrub habitat and pond habitat where Slash Pine, Dahoon Holly and Button Bush preside. This is easy-going for your dog on sand trails all the way. Don't neglect a short detour to a wooden chapel constructed at the edge of the pond in memory of H.E. "Buddy" Long, a scout leader from the 1980s. Depending on the time of year, the shallow depression can be filled and brimming with cranes and egrets and wood ducks or bone dry.

The Geneva Wilderness can also be used as a jumping-off point for the yellow-blazed *Flagler Trail*. This remnant of Henry Flagler's great Florida empire was abandoned in the 1950s and is now a multi-use trail through the scrublands and swamps of Seminole County. From the junction here the trail runs south into the Little Big Econ State Forest.

Seminole County

Phone Number
- (407) 349-0959

Website
- seminolecountyfl.gov/parksrec/naturallands/geneva

Admission Fee
- None

Park Hours
- Dawn to dusk

Directions
- *Geneva*; south of town. From Route 46 take CR 426 and stay on it as it bears right. The park entrance is on the left, past Old Mims Road.

Although the canine hiking in Geneva Wilderness is far from strenuous, your dog will welcome a break at the pondside chapel.

Trail Sense: Park maps and a mapboard reside at the trailhead and directional posts lead the way out on the trail.

Dog Friendliness

Dogs are allowed to enjoy these quiet trails.

Traffic

Horses and bikes are allowed but mostly foot traffic.

Canine Swimming

The flatwoods pond is best saved for the wildlife.

Trail Time

About an hour with more canine hiking available on the *Flagler Trail*.

25

Trimble Park

The Park

Sadie Trimble was 36 years old when her husband died in the flu epidemic of 1918. Left alone with small children she took control of the family's hundreds of acres of citrus groves, becoming a pioneer for women in Central Florida's citrus industry. In 1926 Trimble donated 40 acres slotted between Lake Beauclair and Lake Carlton to Orange County for a park. Residents knew the Trimble land because the community dock on Lake Beauclair, across which moved much of the region's freight was located close by. In 1978 Orange County purchased another 31 acres to complete the 71-acre park that is still bordered by Trimble family groves that offer up that orange fragrance your dog sniffs as she jumps out of the car.

Orange County

Phone Number
- (352) 383-1993

Website
- apps.ocfl.net/dept/CEsrvcs/Parks/ParkDetails.asp?ParkID=40

Admission Fee
- None

Park Hours
- Summer: 8:00 a.m.- 8:00 p.m.; Winter: 8:00 a.m.- 6:00 p.m

Directions
- *Tangerine*; west of town at 5802 Trimble Park Road. From the Orange Blossom Trail, US 441, travel three miles west on Trimble Park Road into the park.

The Walks

The heritage oaks and cypresses, all dressed in their finest Spanish moss, are the stars of Trimble Park. Palms fill in a vibrant understory. The nature trail fills up only a little more than a mile around the peninsula but you will want to walk slowly with your dog to better see the avian cavalcade of eagles, osprey, hawks and shorebirds that come here to gorge. Close to the shore the trees reach out into the lakes like fishing poles. In addition to the flat, paw-friendly natural surfaces for your dog there are sections of finely crushed gravel and a 720-foot boardwalk as well. Even the novice canine hiker will not need a break on the shady Trimble Park trails but your dog will no doubt want to stop at the benches and picnic tables overlooking the water nonetheless.

Trail Sense: Hand-crafted wooden signposts point you around the park.

Dog Friendliness

Dogs are welcome on the trails and in the campground. Poop bags are provided.

Traffic

Foot traffic that is considerably less on weekdays.

Canine Swimming

There is plenty of easy access to the lake waters - which the alligators find useful as well.

Trail Time

Less than an hour.

The Trimble family planted oranges here but they left plenty of majestic palms and oaks for your dog to enjoy.

26
Lake Jesup
Conservation Area

The Park

One of the largest lakes in Central Florida carries the name of Brigadier General Thomas Sidney Jesup, known as the "Father of the Modern Quartermaster Corps." He served as Quartermaster General for 42 years, holding the record for the longest continual service in the same position in U.S. military history. He did leave his desk in Washington to assume command of all American troops in Florida during the Second Seminole War from 1837 until 1842.

The water quality of the lake was so degraded by the 1990s that fish kills were common and the layer of muck on the lake bottom was over nine feet thick. The St. Johns River Water Management District developed a plan for restoration that involved purchasing over 5,000 acres of floodplain and creating the Lake Jesup Conservation Area.

Seminole County

Phone Number
- (386) 329-4404

Website
- sjrwmd.com/recreationguide/lakejesup

Admission Fee
- None

Park Hours
- Dawn to dusk

Directions
- *Oviedo*; north of town. From CR 426, turn north on Van Arsdale Street, west on Florida Avenue and north on Elm Street to the parking area.

The Walks

There are three tracts with hiking trails around Lake Jesup, two on the west and one on the east. The mission of the District is to restore the lake and management of the trails can be spotty at best. This canine hike is through the East Tract, where access is easy and parking plentiful. Your dog's explorations will be on a 2.1-mile balloon trail that was has been closed in the recent past. Tripping through a primordial hammock of twisted oaks and towering cabbage palms, your destination is a sturdy two-story observation tower that your dog can easily clamber up to soak in views of Lake Jesup.

There may be times during the year when you won't need an observation tower to see Lake Jesup - it may be under your feet so take the loop in a counterclockwise direction to assure access to the tower. This is shady, jungle-like canine hiking all the way.

Trail Sense: A few stray trails may throw you off your route - pay close attention to the white blazes and medalions when you can spot them. The tower is on the outside of the loop.

Your dog can climb the wooden steps of the Spanish moss-draped observation tower to look out across Lake Jesup.

Dog Friendliness
Dogs are allowed to explore these trails that evoke Old Florida.

Traffic
Trail users are few and far between.

Canine Swimming
Lake Jesup is considered to have one of the highest concentrations of alligators in Florida.

Trail Time
About an hour.

27
Blue Spring State Park

The Park

Following the Civil War, when Florida tourism was in its infancy, Blue Spring, with its daily discharge of 104 million gallons of 72-degree water, was an early must-see destination. Sightseers would come by rail or ship to Jacksonville and board paddle-wheeled steamboats for journeys up the St. Johns River. The golden age of the river tours was over by the 1880s as the railroads arrived and Florida development pushed southward.

Some visitors never stopped coming to Blue Spring, however. They were manatees, aquatic herbivorous marine mammals that will perish in waters below 60 degrees. Every winter the "sea cows" would migrate to Blue Spring waters, a phenomenon that was captured by French oceanographer Jacques Cousteau is a documentary called *The Forgotten Mermaids* in 1971. The film ignited interest in the gentle creatures and Blue Spring's role as a winter refuge, which greatly influenced the state's decision to establish the 2,643-acre park.

Volusia County

Phone Number
- (386) 775-3663

Website
- floridastateparks.org/bluespring

Admission Fee
- Vehicle parking fee

Park Hours
- 8:00 a.m. to sunset

Directions
- *Orange City*, Take I-4 to US 17/92 to Orange City. Turn west on French Avenue and follow the road until the pavement ends and the park entrance is on the left.

The Walks

There is only one hiking trail in the park but it is a superlative, shady 4.5-mile ramble filled with sabal palms and a Spanish-moss draped mixed forest. Most of the visitors to the park are looking at the manatees so you won't have much competition for this trail before you decide to turn around and retrace your dog's pawprints. Your dog can watch the manatees as well

- dogs are permitted along the 1/3-mile boardwalk that traces Blue Springs Run.

Trail Sense: You can see everywhere you need to go from the parking lot.

Dog Friendliness

Dogs are not allowed in the water or in the rental canoes; dogs can stay in the campground but not in the cabins.

Traffic

The sightseer boardwalk is a crowded space but the canine hiking will likely be a mostly solitary affair.

Canine Swimming

None.

Trail Time

The pioneer-era Thursby House was constructed with the finest of materials and stands much as it did 130 years ago.

You can spend up to a half-day on the *Pine Island Trail* if you hike with your dog to its conclusion at a primitive campsite near the St. Johns River.

28
Pete's Preserve

The Park

Lake-Sumter Community College received a special appropriation from the Florida Legislature to construct this maze of footpaths around the campus sinkhole and deep water pond, which was dedicated in 1990. Twenty years later the nature trail on the Leesburg campus was named for biology professor Pete Kehde who retired after 32 years in the classroom. Kehde lobbied for the creation of a living laboratory for students that would also be a beautiful setting for the entire community.

The Walks

Pete's Preserve is one of the best places to hike with your dog and get a nature education. You won't go more than a few steps without encountering a placard describing a new plant. The mulched, paw-friendly trails snake through a transitional area between the woodlands and the wetlands. The boardwalk with observation tower is a highlight at Pete's Preserve. The boards have been routed to slide past a

Lake County

Phone Number
- None

Website
- lscc.edu

Admission Fee
- None

Park Hours
- Dawn to dusk

Directions
- *Leesburg*; east of town on the Lake-Sumter Community College campus at 9501 US Highway 441. Take College Drive north off US 441 and turn right into the campus before the sports complex. Parking for the trailhead is behind the Everett A. Kelly Convocation Center.

The start of your dog's hiking day at Pete's Preserve.

bald cypress and pond cypress that dominate the center of the wetlands. After you are through exploring Pete's Preserve you can also exercise your dog on the half-mile paved track around the sports complex and visit the fenced-in Leesburg Dog Park in a large field across College Drive.

Trail Sense: There is a map posted at the trail entrance and directional posts in the Preserve.

The mulched trails take your dog through the transition from forest to marsh at Pete's Preserve.

Dog Friendliness
Dogs are welcome to enjoy Pete's Preserve.

Traffic
Foot traffic only.

Canine Swimming
Nope.

Trail Time
Less than an hour.

29
Lake Griffin
State Park

The Park

The nine interconnected lakes known today as the Harris Chain cover approximately 50,000 acres of water. The depth of the lakes is about 10-12 feet on average with no reefs or open lake obstacles to impede navigation. Big Lake Harris has the deepest water at about 30 feet along the south shoreline. Lake Griffin is the shallowest and sports the least amount of development.

These gentle waters have attracted settlement for thousands of years. The land was used for farming and citrus groves through the 1930s until the State purchased 383 acres 1946. In 1968 a camping a boating park was opened along the Dead River Marsh here, which connects the boat dock to Lake Griffin.

Lake County

Phone Number
- (352) 360-6760

Website
- floridastateparks.org/lakegriffin

Admission Fee
- Vehicle parking fee, although you can park outside the park toll booth and walk your dog in at a reduced rate

Park Hours
- 8:00 a.m. to sunset

Directions
- *Fruitland Park*; at 3089 Highway 441-27. From Leesburg go north from the intersection with SR 44 to the park entrance on the right.

The Walks

Lake Griffin State Park is not a hotbed of canine hiking but if you are looking for a low-key park to enjoy camping, boating, fishing and picnicking with your dog this is the place. The park nature trail can be conquered in 20 minutes and is one of the most informative of its genre. Highlights include superb examples of Florida's state tree, the sabal palm, and resurrection ferns growing on overhanging branches. The paw-friendly path skips past the edge of the freshwater marsh and onto a hardwood hammock as it illustrates the contrast of plant and animal life found at different elevations. As the trail crosses the campground it reaches the high point of 85 feet in the park and your dog will have achieved a 25-foot elevation gain from the marsh.

Trail Sense: A park map provides orientation for the *Nature Trail* and the interpretive route is well-signed.

Dog Friendliness

Dogs are allowed on the trails and in the campground.

Traffic

Just a bit of foot traffic is all.

Canine Swimming

Alligators may be present should your dog look to cool off near the boat ramp.

Trail Time

Less than an hour.

Lake Griffin's signature live oak is Florida's fifth largest.

30
Fleet Peeples Park

The Park

Fleetwood Peeples was born in Varnille, South Carolina in 1898. He came to Florida in 1922 as the swimming instructor at Rollins College and stayed for 50 years. In that time Peeples, who was also the official naturalist for Rollins and the City of Winter Park, taught some 20,000 children to swim by his method of "loving them across the lake." Peeples passed at the age of 95 and this park is his legacy.

The Walks

There isn't much hiking to be had in this small lakeside park but there is no better place in Central Florida to bring your water-loving dog for a good time. Thirteen of the park's 23 acres are set aside as off-leash territory for your dog, including a stretch of sandy beach on Lake Baldwin, EXCEPT on weekends from 10:00 a.m. until 4:00 p.m. And when your dog has had his fill of dog-paddling and fetching in the lake there is a small maze of shady trails in the fenced-in area. Don't be surprised if you are joined by dogs from any direction as you hike with your dog here.

Orange County

Phone Number
- (407) 599-3334

Website
- ffpp.org/

Admission Fee
- A $75 annual fee per dog was repealed in the Spring of 2011 and the dog park is free - for now

Park Hours
- 8:00 a.m. to sunset

Directions
- *Winter Park*; at 2000 South Lakemont Avenue. From I-4 take Colonial Drive (Route 50/92/17) east to Maguire Boulevard and turn left. Follow the road as it becomes New Broad Street and turn left on Jake Street just before Lake Baldwin. Turn right on Lakemont Avenue and continue to the lakeshore park on the right.

Happy dogs are everywhere in Fleet Peeples Park.

Bonus - The Perfect Dog Bath

Fleet Peeples Park has two elevated dog wash stations to spruce up before you leave. A proper dog bath is key to maintaining your pet's vigorous good health. The skin is the body's largest organ and a perfect dog bath is key to stimulating blood circulation and keeping the skin healthy. Improper bathing can cause a matted condition in the coat which is uncomfortable to your dog. The first step in the perfect dog bath is a good brushing.

For short-haired dogs brush in a circular motion with a curry comb made of rubber with teeth cut into the edges. It will pull the dead coat out. Slicker brushes will take out the dead undercoat. Start on the legs and hold the outer hair so that you can brush from the skin outward. If it is not removed, the coat will easily mat. Use this technique all over the dog - legs, body and tail. Dogs resent the tail being brushed so save it for last. For fine-haired dogs use a natural bristle brush. Moisten the area to be worked with a good coat conditioner.

For long-haired dogs use a pin brush if the coat is not tangled, a slicker brush if the coat is tangled. Start at the legs, again brushing from the skin out and brushing only a few hairs at a time. The secret to thorough brushing is to brush only a few hairs at a time. Check each area with a comb; if the comb goes through without stress continue all the way up to the middle of the dog's back. Go to the loin area and to the back legs; then move to each side of the back of the dog.

You are now ready to wash. Never use human shampoos to wash your dog. Dog shampoos are specially formulated to match the pH level of a dog's skin. Human shampoos can strip a dog's coat of essential oils. The right way to bathe a dog is determined by the texture and length of the coat. Short-haired dogs are washed with a vigorous circular motion which will pull out the dirt. On dogs with a medium-length coast, use a back-and-forth motion. As the hair gets longer, go only in the direction the hair grows.

Step 1. Rinse the dog completely.

Step 2. Apply the shampoo along the back, working up as much lather as possible; do the same with the belly, legs and tail.

Step 3. Rinse the coat with one hand to run water on the dog and the other hand in a kneading fashion to work the soap out. Make certain all the soap is out as dried soap will dull a coat and cause skin problems.

Step 4. Before towel-drying, squeeze as much water out of the coat as possible by pulling the hair straight out and squeezing at the same time.

Step 5. Use a washcloth to clean the dog's face and avoid getting water in his ears. Moisture inside ears provides conditions for fungus infections.

Step 6. Towel dry your dog and use a hand-held hair dryer on thick-coated dogs but never use a human hair dryer as they run too hot and can burn the dog and damage the coat.

Voila! A clean, healthy dog.

And because sometimes
the best hikes with your
dog do not take
take place on dirt and
grass...

31.
A Walking Tour of Downtown Orlando

1.   Lake Eola Park
North Rosalind Avenue

This small lake is actually an 80-foot deep sinkhole. In 1883 Jacob Summerlin donated land around the lake to the city on the condition it be developed as park with trees planted and a "driveway" installed around the lake, which his sons named after a woman they knew. Summerlin's gift came attached with a nebulous string - should the city ever fail to keep the park beautiful in the opinion of Summerlin or his heirs the land would revert back to the family.

Jacob Summerlin was born in Alachua County on February 20, 1820 and often claimed to be the first white child born in Florida under American rule. His early fortune came running cattle across the vast stretches of Central Florida where he was known as the "King of the Crackers," after the long whips used to drive the cows. He lived until 1893, long enough to see the park officially dedicated in 1892. The swans that ruled the lake were descendants of a pair imported from the private preserves of King Edward VII of England in 1910, named Mr. and Mrs. Bill. Legend maintains that Mister drowned the missus after a setting of eggs failed to hatch. When Mr. Bill finally died at the age of 78 he was mounted and put on display in the Chamber of Commerce building.

The lake's landmark fountain was installed in 1912 at the cost of $10,000. It was replaced in 1957 with a $350,000 model and after lightning struck the fountain in 2009 the tab for new water jets was $2.3 million.

WALK OVER TO THE CORNER OF WALL STREET AND ROSALIND AVENUE. ON THE NORTHWEST CORNER, TO YOUR RIGHT, IS...

2.   First Church of Christ Scientist
24 North Rosalind Avenue

George Foote Dunham was born in Iowa in 1876 and schooled in Chicago architecture before moving to Portland, Oregon in 1907. He worked throughout the midwest for more than twenty years, best known for his residential work, but with important public buildings on his resume as well. A Christian Scientist, Dunham relocated to Orlando in 1928 to build the congregation's first meetinghouse; it had organized a decade before. Dunham designed a Neoclassical Greek temple in a crucifix form. The Christian Scientists left the building in 1975 and it was purchased by the St. George Orthodox Church.

WALK DOWN WALL STREET TO ITS END ONE BLOCK AWAY.
IN FRONT OF YOU IS...

3. Old Orange County Courthouse
65 East Central Boulevard at Magnolia Avenue

Pennsylvania-born Murry S. King migrated to Orlando at the age of 34 in 1904. He became Florida's first registered architect and a leader in crafting a Central Florida style of architecture suited to the region. The elegant Neoclassical courthouse, the sixth to serve Orange County, was his final and best known project. Constructed of variegated Indiana limestone on a rusticated base with Tuscan colonnades, the building was completed by King's son, James, after he passed away in 1925. The building is now the home of the Orange County Regional History Center.

TURN LEFT ON MAGNOLIA AVENUE.

4. Orlando Public Library
101 East Central Boulevard at Magnolia Avenue

Books were lent in Orlando via private libraries until May 11, 1920 when a referendum for a public library passed with a vote of 417 to 19. The foundation for the new collection came from the personal library of Charles L. Albertson, a retired police inspector from New York City. The Albertson Public Library opened in 1923. In 1964 the town's first public library was demolished and construction begun on the current building designed as "a composition in monolithic concrete" by New Canaan, Connecticut architect John M. Johansen. The monolith would grow even larger with an expansion to 290,000 square feet filling the entire block in the 1980s. Today the Orlando Public Library is the largest public library building in the State of Florida.

5. Rogers Building
37-39 South Magnolia Avenue

Gordon Rogers sailed from England for Florida in 1883 but he wasn't quite ready to put the Mother Country behind him. He searched the state for a spot where he could erect a fashionable English gentleman's club and alighted here in 1886. Architect William H. Mullins created a picturesque Queen Anne building with a corner tower using pine and cypress boards covered with stucco. Over the years Rogers imported pressed zinc panels from England to cover the stucco and give his clubhouse the appearance of carved stone. In 1926 Arthur M. Higgins purchased the building for $80,000 and did a complete interior and exterior remodeling. He kept the zinc panels, however, and even purchased the building next door and covered it with the same panels.

6. First United Methodist Church of Orlando
142 East Jackson Street at Magnolia Avenue

Circuit-riding preachers added Orlando to their routes in the 1840s but it was not until 1882 that the town's Methodists constructed a church on this location. The current classically inspired, gleaming white sanctuary, raised in 1962, is the third used by the congregation that now numbers over 3,000 members.

TURN RIGHT ON SOUTH STREET.

7. Orlando City Hall
400 South Orange Avenue at South Street

The winner of Orlando's design competition for a new city hall backed out of the project in a dispute over fees so a consortium of companies was cobbled together to execute the design by Heller & Leake, a San Francisco firm. The exterior of the nine-story government center is clad in precast concrete instead of costly stone, except for a few granite accents. The copper dome is decorative and does not reflect a great domed hall below. Revenue from the adjacent office towers was expected to defray the $32 million tab for City Hall that was finished in 1992.

8. City Hall Tower of Light
South Street at Orange Avenue

The 60-foot tower of laminated plate glass and stainless steel was sculpted in 1992 by Ed Carpenter of Portland, Oregon, an artist specializing in large-scale public installations. The tower is illuminated at three different levels by computerized lights.

TURN RIGHT ON ORANGE AVENUE AND WALK UP TO
CHURCH STREET.

9. First National Bank and Trust Company
190 South Orange Avenue at Church Street

Howard M. Reynolds was an Orlando architect at ease with the fashionable styles of the 1920s and 1930s, including Mediterranean Revival, Colonial Revival, Spanish Colonial, Egyptian Revival, Art Deco and Art Moderne. Here he blended a dash of Egyptian flavor into his Art Deco design on the gracefully symmetrical bank vault for the First National Bank. The building opened in 1930 but the bank failed shortly thereafter at the height of the Depression. It reorganized again on Valentine's Day 1934.

TURN LEFT ON CHURCH STREET.

10. Kress Store
15 West Church Street

Samuel H. Kress opened his first "stationery and notions" store in Nanticoke, Pennsylvania in 1887 and established his chain of S. H. Kress & Co. 5-10-25 Cent Stores in 1896. Kress pictured his stores as works of public art that would enhance a town streetscape and a century later his buildings are indeed cherished long after his merchandising has disappeared. In the 1930s the company embraced the emerging Art Deco style and head architect Edward Sibbert would go on to design more than 50 stores in the decorative style, making liberal use of colorful terra cotta, and employing strong verticals that would rise to the letters "Kress," often in gold letters, at the roofline. This is one of Sibbert's designs, opened in 1936.

11. Old Orlando Railroad Depot
76 West Church Street

The Lake Monroe and Orlando Railroad was organized in 1875 with a charter to build from the St. Johns River port of Sanford south to Orlando. The South Florida Railroad was incorporated on October 16, 1878 and rolled into town on November 11, 1880. The first passengers disembarked at a temporary wooden station run from the Bumby Warehouse across the tracks. Orlando was just a stopping point for the railroad, however. The line was in a race to the Gulf of Mexico at Tampa, which it eventually won. In 1890 the South Florida constructed a proper Victorian passenger station and it remained a busy platform until 1926 when it became a freight station and ticket outlet. Its life of railroad service ended in 1972. On the tracks beside the platform is "Old Duke," a 1912 Baldwin steam engine.

12. Bumby Block
102-110 West Church Street

Joseph Bumby arrived in town from Colchester, England in 1873 and began peddling hay and grain and fertilizer from a warehouse on this site. Bumby had a bit of railroading experience in his background and when the South Florida Railroad arrived in Orlando in 1880 he became the line's first freight and ticket agent and ran the first depot out of his store. In 1886 Bumby went into the hardware business and constructed this building. The slogan "If you can't find it - go to Bumby's" resonated throughout Orlando until 1966. It now anchors the Church Street Station entertainment complex.

13. Orlando Hotel
129 West Church Street

This building began life as William Slemon's dry goods store. In 1924 the frame building was replaced with the current brick structure that retains such architectural details as pressed metal ceilings and a green tile awning on the second floor.

TURN RIGHT ON GARLAND AVENUE. TURN RIGHT ON PINE STREET.

14. Carey Hand Building
36 West Pine Street

Carey Hand, a trained embalmer, joined his father's undertaking business located down the street in 1907. He bought his father out in 1914 and in 1918 he had this building constructed to house his mortuary. Local architect F.H. Trimble designed the funeral home with a Tuscan flavor behind an entryway of arches and paired columns. Hand would construct the first crematorium in the South and his funeral home was the first in the state to have a chapel. Hand operated the business until 1947 serving a five-county area as the largest funeral home in Central Florida.

15. Tinker Building
18 West Pine Street

Three years after leaving the sandlots of Kansas as a 19-year old, Joseph Bert Tinker was playing shortstop for the Chicago Cubs in 1902. Before the decade was out Tinker would play on four pennant-winning and two World Championship Cub teams - the last the franchise has had in over 100 years. Joe Tinker was elected to Baseball's Hall of Fame in 1946, as much for a famous bit of doggerel called "Baseball's Sad Lexicon" that celebrated the exploits of Cub infielders "Tinker to Evers to Chance" written in 1910 by New York sports writer Franklin P. Adams as for his play on the field. After his playing days were over Tinker came to Orlando in 1921 to manage the Florida State League Orlando Tigers and got caught up in the Florida land boom. He ran his real estate business from this building he constructed in 1925. Tinker helped make Orlando a spring training destination and for 75 years minor league baseball was played in Joe Tinker Field, a stadium the city built to honor the former Cub shortstop.

16. Elijah Hand Building
15-17 West Hand Street

Elijah Hand arrived in Orlando from Indiana in 1885; he was the second undertaker in town and the first embalmer. Hand briefly forged a partnership with that first undertaker, E.A. Richards, but was on his own by 1890 making coffins and furniture and running a livery. Hand had this building with decorative brickwork that can still be seen on the second floor constructed in 1905.

17. Orlando Federal Savings & Loan Association Building
100 South Orange Avenue at Pine Street

This was the third of Orlando's original trio of 1920s skyscrapers, constructed in 1924. It follows the traditional form to raise early skyscrapers in the style of a classic Greek column with a defined base (the two-story classically framed openings), a shaft (the unadorned brick central floors) and a capital (the braided arched windows and decorative cornice). After the bank failed Henry Metcalf, a real-estate investor, bought the building in 1930 for $125,000.

CROSS OVER ORANGE STREET.

18. Ellis Building
35 East Pine Street

James L. Giles had this modest brick building constructed as speculative property in the 1880s, early in his banking career. Giles would become mayor of Orlando in 1916 and become the first chief city executive to serve more than one term when he was re-elected in 1924 and again in 1928. William Ellis gave the building a complete makeover when he purchased it in 1925; the upper stories have remained unaltered since.

19. Orange County Building and Loan Society
38 East Pine Street at Court Street

The association organized in 1921 and set up shop across the street. In 1928 it moved into this Mediterranean Revival structure on the corner.

TURN LEFT ON COURT AVENUE. TURN LEFT ON CENTRAL AVENUE.

20. Yowell-Duckworth Building
1 South Orange Avenue at Central Avenue

Newton Yowell came with his family to Orlando from Luray, Virginia in 1884 at the age of 13, hoping the warm air would cure his father's tuberculosis. It didn't and Yowell was soon clerking in a local dry goods store. In October of 1894 he borrowed $2,000 to open his small dry goods store. That winter's freeze crippled the Orlando economy and Yowell was one of the few merchants to stick it out and he soon prospered. In 1913 he partnered with shoe salesman Eugene Duckworth and set out to build a 20th century department store in Orlando and they hired architect Murry S. King to design the four-story emporium. By 1920, he added stores in Apopka, Sanford, Daytona Beach and West Palm Beach. Times were good enough to add a fifth floor and a department store operated here until the 1960s.

21. Dickson-Ives Building
2 South Orange Avenue at Central Avenue

H.H. Dickson and Sidney Ives each came to Orlando in the 1880s and set up mercantile businesses. Dickson sold seed and fertilizer and Ives peddled groceries. In the economic wake of the Great Freeze of 194-95, seven of Orange County's banks shuttered and most of its other businesses shut down as well. Two that soldiered on were Dickson and Ives. The two formed a partnership in 1897 and began selling groceries. In 1914 after remodeling their building on this site their business re-emerged as a full service department store. That building was demolished in 1920 and replaced with this structure that blended classical elements with tropical themes. The Dickson-Ives business would operate until 1965.

22. State Bank of Orlando and Trust Company
1 North Orange Street

Philadelphia-born Louis Conrad Massey came to Orlando with a University of Pennsylvania law degree in tow in 1885. When the State Bank of Orlando was formed in 1893 Massey was its president and guided the enterprise until his death. In 1919 the bank purchased the prime northeast corner of Orange Avenue and Central Boulevard and planned the town's second skyscraper. William L. Stoddart, a New York architect who specialized in big downtown hotels, delivered a Neoclassical design for the ten-story high-rise. Look up to see decorative terra cotta panels. The bank closed in 1929 and the Florida Bank at Orlando moved into the quarters in 1933 and stayed until 1972 when the building became the property of Orange County.

TURN RIGHT ON NORTH ORANGE STREET.

23. Angebilt Hotel
37 North Orange Avenue

Joseph Fenner Ange was a general contractor from North Carolina who came to Orlando in 1913. He scored a major commission to build the Yowell-Duckworth store and by 1921 he was able to sink a million dollars into this hotel, designed by Murry S. King. Ange would sell his interest in the hotel two months after it opened in 1923. In its day the 250-room Angebilt was the town's leading hotel. It also hosted two radio stations.

24. Rose Building
49 North Orange Avenue

Georgia-born Walter Washington Rose began his working life as a Western Union operator. Telegraph business brought him to Orlando in 1909 and he soon quit and entered the real estate business in 1913 with $25. He began by developing land on East Central Avenue. In 1924 he constructed this building, designed by Murry S. King, as headquarters for his Central Florida Development Company. The Mediterranean Revival structure was supposed to be the base for a ten-story office building but those plans never materialized. Look up to see a medallion with a stylized rendering of the name "Rose." Walter Rose would go on to serve in the Florida state senate from 1932 until 1949.

25. Rutland's
63 North Orange Avenue

This sleek Art Moderne structure was designed by F. Earl Deloe in 1938. Joseph Rutland purchased it in 1940 for his clothing store which operated here until the late 1960s. in 1952 Rutland added three non-conforming stories which later remodelings have attempted to incorporate into the original design.

LOOK NORTH UP ORANGE STREET TO THE STAIR-STEP TOWER...

26. Bank of America Center
390 North Orange Avenue

This building is all there is to show for the largest development scheme ever to hit Orlando. It was the vision of William duPont III in 1984 to populate six blocks of Orange Avenue with three beefy office towers, a 650-room luxury hotel, scads of retail space and restaurants and parking for 4,000 cars. This 28-story tower for First Federal Association Savings and Loan was ready by 1988 but that is as far as DuPont Center ever got after its backer suffered financial reversals.

TURN RIGHT ON JEFFERSON STREET.

27. U.S. Post Office and Courthouse
northwest corner of Jefferson Street and Magnolia Avenue

Orlando did not have a dedicated post office building until 1917 and this grander model came along in 1941. Louis A. Simon, a government architect gave the building a restrained Italian Renaissance design.

TURN RIGHT ON MAGNOLIA AVENUE.

28. Cathedral of St. Luke
130 North Magnolia Avenue

In October 1892, General Convention set apart the Missionary Jurisdiction of South Florida, and William Crane Gray was elected and consecrated first Bishop. Bishop Gray made Orlando his home and St. Luke's was designated as the Cathedral Church for South Florida on March 31, 1902. In 1922 the existing frame cathedral was moved across the church property to make room for this Gothic Revival sanctuary. Unfortunately the design by Boston architects Frohman, Robb and Little, creators of the National Cathedral in Washington, was not fully realized due to the crash of the Florida land boom. The church was dedicated on Easter 1926.

TURN LEFT ON WASHINGTON STREET AND WALK ONE BLOCK TO THE TOUR STARTING POINT IN LAKE EOLA PARK.

Index to Parks
Around Orlando...

Index To Parks By County

"I can't think of anything that brings me closer to tears than when my old dog - completely exhausted after a hard day in the field - limps away from her nice spot in front of the fire and comes over to where I'm sitting and puts her head in my lap, a paw over my knee, and closes her eyes, and goes back to sleep. I don't know what I've done to deserve that kind of friend."
-Gene Hill

Parks Alphabetically

page

Other Books On Hiking With Your Dog from Cruden Bay Books
www.hikewithyourdog.com

DOGGIN' AMERICA: 100 Ideas For Great Vacations To Take With Your Dog - $19.95

DOGGIN' THE MID-ATLANTIC: 400 Tail-Friendly Parks To Hike With Your Dog In New Jersey, Pennsylvania, Delaware, Maryland and Northern Virginia - $18.95

DOGGIN' CLEVELAND: The 50 Best Places To Hike With Your Dog In Northeast Ohio - $12.95

DOGGIN' PITTSBURGH: The 50 Best Places To Hike With Your Dog In Southeast Pennsylvania - $12.95

DOGGIN' ATLANTA: The 50 Best Places To Hike With Your Dog in North Georgia - $12.95

DOGGIN' NORTHWEST FLORIDA: The 50 Best Places To Hike With Your Dog In The Panhandle - $12.95

DOGGIN' ASHEVILLE: The 30 Best Places To Hike With Your Dog in Western Carolina - $9.95

DOGGIN' THE POCONOS: The 33 Best Places To Hike With Your Dog In Pennsylvania's Northeast Mountains - $9.95

DOGGIN' THE BERKSHIRES: The 33 Best Places To Hike With Your Dog In Western Massachusetts - $9.95

DOGGIN' NORTHERN VIRGINIA: The 50 Best Places To Hike With Your Dog In NOVA - $9.95

DOGGIN' DELAWARE: The 40 Best Places To Hike With Your Dog In The First State - $9.95

DOGGIN' MARYLAND: The 100 Best Places To Hike With Your Dog In The Free State - $12.95

DOGGIN' JERSEY: The 100 Best Places To Hike With Your Dog In The Garden State - $12.95

DOGGIN' RHODE ISLAND: The 25 Best Places To Hike With Your Dog In The Ocean State - $7.95

DOGGIN' MASSACHUSETTS: The 100 Best Places To Hike With Your Dog in the Bay State - $12.95

DOGGIN' CONNECTICUT: The 57 Best Places To Hike With Your Dog In The Nutmeg State - $12.95

DOGGIN' THE FINGER LAKES: The 50 Best Places To Hike With Your Dog - $12.95

DOGGIN' LONG ISLAND: The 30 Best Places To Hike With Your Dog In New York's Playground - $9.95

DOGGIN' THE TIDEWATER: The 33 Best Places To Hike With Your Dog from the Northern Neck to Virginia Beach - $9.95

DOGGIN' THE CAROLINA COASTS: The 50 Best Places To Hike With Your Dog Along The North Carolina And South Carolina Shores - $11.95

DOGGIN' AMERICA'S BEACHES: A Traveler's Guide To Dog-Friendly Beaches - $12.95

THE CANINE HIKER'S BIBLE - $19.95

A Bark In The Park: The 55 Best Places To Hike With Your Dog In The Philadelphia Region - $12.95

A Bark In The Park: The 50 Best Places To Hike With Your Dog In The Baltimore Region - $12.95

A Bark In The Park: The 37 Best Places To Hike With Your Dog In Pennsylvania Dutch Country - $9.95

Made in the USA
Monee, IL
13 January 2020